Think this,
Not that

It's time to update your conventional wisdom

CHET W. SISK

Jasina Media WorldWide LLC
Denver, Colorado

Think This, Not That is published by Jasina Media WorldWide LLC

Cover design by Nivesh Rawathal www.behance.net/NiveshR

Book design by Black Cat Creative Services, Cleveland, OH

Library of Congress Cataloging-in-Publication Data
Sisk, Chet W.
        Think this, not that: It's time to update your conventional
        wisdom / Chet W. Sisk
        197 pp
        1. Self-help.   2. Positive thinking.   3. Homeless.

ISBN: 978-0-615-40662-6

Contents

Acknowledgements

I give special thanks to…

To the creator of all things for putting these words on my heart.

To my old and new friends in Namibia, Malaysia, Spain and South Africa: Juliet, Brian, Hera, Hanaan, "Smiley", Gabriel and Nivesh, The World Assembly of Youth and The San People of the Kalahari Desert.

To my sister organizations – Loving Hugs through Wendy Clark and Same Café in Denver, CO.

To writers Damali Ayo, David Givens, and Maurice Howard for fostering the spirit of authorship in the family.

To Dr. Paul Hamilton, whose book *Shattering The Myths* started me down the path to asking questions about everything. *No sacred cows!*

My mom and grandmother for always holding the space and loving me.

My siblings who kept me in check while I was growing up.

To Michelle, for being a good friend.

To Angela, for listening to me rant and rave.

My sons Chase Maliq and Chet Mario for bringing up the rear.

My editor, Jill Scott Conklin, who is just one of the coolest people in the world.

And to my long-time friend Opalanga Pugh who transitioned this year.

Krik, krak, krout. I've got this story out.

sk

Introduction

I have been a volunteer Life Skills teacher at The Samaritan House Homeless Shelter in Denver, Colorado for almost 10 years. Contrary to the suspicions of some of my students, I am not there because I am fulfilling a court-ordered community-service obligation or on some work release program. I am there because I discovered my calling in life— to serve others in personal, spiritual and social transition.

I had to be dragged kicking and screaming into this life calling thing through the bankruptcy of my advertising agency and my divorce, thus, losing everything. I started volunteering because I had time on my hand and nowhere to go. Some people have a much more romantic story of finding their life calling. Mine—*not so much.*

My job at the shelter was to teach the students basics in job interviewing techniques and resume writing. At least, that's how it started off. My first year there was uneventful, except for my frustration around many of the students who would graduate from my 90-day class would return to homelessness. I truly understand how care workers can get compassion burnout. You put in all of this time in with people you're hoping will become productive citizens only to realize you're really just spinning your wheels.

6

Then, after some observation, I realized something rather basic. Despite the new skills the students acquired from the class, what the students spoke about when they were leaving the shelter—what they believed to be true—was the same as when they first arrived. In a moment of clarity I realized we may have given them new skills, but we did not help them change their belief system.

One of my students asked me "what is one thing you know for sure after spending so much time doing this class?" It's a no-brainer: garbage in, garbage out. If our beliefs are faulty, the outcome of our actions is usually faulty or at best, would remain the same.

Bad policy, bad decisions, bad law, bad governance, bad manners and maybe even bad breath can come from bad beliefs. Imagine what would happen if we would draw from better information?

An occasional Tic Tac wouldn't hurt either.

To be fair, many of the students over the years knew the power of personal affirmations from things like *The Secret* or watching Oprah or the latest from Eckhart Tolle or some new thought/Bible-based concept of "name it and claim it." But after watching these students over a period of time, I realized that a positive mental attitude wasn't enough to change the nasty experiences many of them were having.

I took this high churn/recidivism rate on as a personal challenge. *How can we do better?* Then, I started paying attention to some of the things the students were saying as part of the collective class. They were saying things that

7

everyone knew and agreed to. It's what we call "conventional wisdom."

Conventional wisdom is a term used to describe ideas or explanations that are generally accepted as true by the public. Things like, "Nice guys finish last" or, "Rich people are greedy" or, "The early bird gets the worm," are all these little "Gospelettes" we all tell each other and agree are true. That wouldn't be so bad except for one thing: most of our conventional wisdom is inaccurate.

Let me come back to that point in just a second....

With my students, I noticed that their *group conventional wisdom* frequently trumped their *personal beliefs.* One moment, a student would pull me aside and tell me, individually, something like this:

"I believe I can do great things."

Then, in a class setting, they would agree to the stated conventional wisdom of the group:

"Life's a bitch, and then you die."

In my previous life in advertising, this kind of group think was what we leveraged to sell product. We understood the power of peer *suggestion* and how our desire to fit in would often beat out personal convictions.. Most of us do this kind of compromise all day long. Don't get me wrong, compromise is not a bad thing. *Compromise using bad data is.*

In one class, I decided to write down some of the conventional wisdom sayings shared by the students. By doing just a little bit of research, I discovered something pretty basic—most conventional wisdom we use today is either outdated, inconsistent, or just plain untrue.

Sooooo...following that logic, a good argument can be made that a lot of the thinking that we draw on to make decisions today is either outdated, inconsistent or just plain untrue. The inevitable outcome puts a cap on our world of possibilities.

It's pretty clear there's a problem in our collective wisdom as a country and in many countries around the world. Our financial, religious, political and social structures are way past being in trouble. My snapshot of society at the shelter made me see the destructiveness of garbage in/garbage out.

And before you dismiss people in transition as not quite being representative of the rest of us, let me assure you that on any particular day, 1/4 to 1/3 of the classes I taught were made up of people who were laid off from IBM, HP, college graduates, former managers and professionals.

To counter the current conventional wisdom tyranny, I decided to take some of the best known conventional wisdom sayings and match them with updated and more accurate counters. Then, I wanted to put these updated ideas to work in the lives of people in the most difficult circumstances in our society—adults going through homelessness and transition. My thinking is that if these tools can work in the most challenging circumstances, they could work for all of us. I also brought in college-level higher thought to the class room. I covered everything from

Quantum Physics to Zen philosophy to Superstring theory, to spirituality, modern politics and world affairs. Instead of teaching down to the students, I challenged them to come up. This expanded their capacity beyond survival mode. I didn't use big, fancy words to show off my education. I made every class tangible, clear and accessible without dumbing down the material. After all, isn't that the point of education?

I called this approach "The Window Effect Method". We're all presented with regular windows of opportunity. The question is, will we look through that window and watch life pass us by, or will we go through that window into a new world of more possibilities?

Sure enough, from my 6-month observational study in 2007, students who went to my class were much more likely not to return to homelessness or slip into homelessness as a way of life.

That success is the genesis of this book.

I will say, there was one other motivation I had. Out of curiosity, I went to one of those personal development weekend seminars with a very well known motivational speaker. He was going to give me the "secret" of how to be successful and become enlightened. The information was cool, but the price for this information was over $1,500 for the weekend. Fortunately, I had a few people who sponsored me out of the goodness of their heart. The $1,500 price is fine if you've got sponsors or have that kind of loot laying around, *but what happens if you don't?*

Does this mean that poor people won't be able to become enlightened? Will only a few people of a certain income bracket achieve self actualization? It seemed as though this codification of enlightenment knowledge was going down the same path of so many things in our society—to the haves and away from the have nots. There seemed to be something fundamentally wrong with that. My belief is that true enlightenment must be *accessible* to everyone, otherwise it's just another version of everything that already exists. This approach I've designed was constructed to be accessible throughout the entire socioeconomic structure—rich and poor, young and old, cool and uncool, *anywhere in the world.*

Unlike Abraham Maslow's Hierarchy of Needs model that says self-actualization occurs at the top of his pyramid of needs and is accessible only to the few, the "Sisk Hierarchy of Empowerment" model says self-actualization is most possible at the point of impact—right at the bottom. When all hell breaks loose, people need new ideas, expanded capacity and a new vision. Otherwise, people will keep recycling the same life or crumble under the weight of it all.

And, unlike many critics, I do not think conventional wisdom is a bad thing. The idea of shared wisdom that allows us to make better collective decisions about the world around us is, I believe, a *good* thing. However, it just may be time for us to do an update of those conventions and ask ourselves three basic questions:

1. Is this idea true?

2. Does this idea serve our individual good?

3. Does this idea serve the greater good?

This book asks these questions. I'll share my experiences of working with homeless people through my Life Skills class at the shelter and how the students responded to this new information. I'll also provide the latest research on some of these new ideas so you can check them out for yourself.

The title of this book came to me on a trip to Frankfurt.. I picked up a *Men's Health Magazine* and saw an article called "Eat This/Not That." It was simple, to the point and gave you exactly what you needed. My hope is that this book is written in that same spirit for both my students at the shelter and for you.

Shift Tools

I am a Journalism School graduate (SIU Salukis—Go Dawgs!), with a background as a television reporter, a radio talk show host and ran my own advertising agency. I take the liberty to share some tools from those previous lives as helps. These tools are real world, practical instruments that can help you shift your thinking to make room for expanded ideas and concepts you may never have otherwise entertained. I've tried them in working with my students in the shelter to see how they work. You'll find them helpful if you're looking for a new approach to some old problems. Besides that, they will help you so that you don't embarrass yourself at your next convention speech, or date, or wine tasting by spouting old ideas that are not true or are wrong.

Thanks for being strong enough to take up reading this book that may challenge your core beliefs about life as you know it. And for those of you who would rather hold onto your current conventional wisdom because "that's the way we've always done it," remember, the first step in healing is admitting that you have a problem!

Altruism

#1. Think this: Pay your goodness forward. Not that: It's important to give back to the community.

At the shelter, we would often experience the "big media event" surrounding someone or some organization making a large contribution of food or clothes or something. I don't want to sound like a "hater" about people giving back to the community, but let me offer something even better.

Pay it forward.

A lot of people think Paying it Forward and Giving Back are the same thing. The difference between the two is that giving back is a single, individual act centered around what the giver is doing. Paying it forward capitalizes on a social network that creates an atmosphere for both giver *and receiver* to participate in goodness. Even more, paying it forward develops an ongoing legacy of giving as a way of life, not as a separate, high profile event.

The current science out there says paying it forward is contagious and that it spreads from person to person to person. When people benefit from kindness they "pay it forward" by helping others who were not originally involved, and this creates a cascade of cooperation that influences bunches more in a social network.

I recently read a brilliant article by researchers James Fowler and Nicholas Christakis. They discovered that when one person gives money to help others in a role-playing game where people have the opportunity to cooperate with each other, the recipients are more likely to give their own money away to other people in future games. This creates a domino effect in which one person's generosity spreads first to three people and then to the nine people that those three people interact with in the future, and then to still other individuals in subsequent waves of the experiment. Christakis says, "The network functions like a matching grant."

From a scientific perspective, these findings suggest the possibility that the process of contagion may have contributed to the evolution of cooperation: Groups with altruists in them will be more altruistic as a whole and more likely to survive than selfish groups

Christakis says, "Our work over the past few years... has led us to conclude that there is a deep and fundamental connection between social networks and goodness. The flow of good and desirable properties like ideas, love and kindness is required for human social networks to endure, and, in turn, networks are required for such properties to spread." And to think all of this happened before the invention of Facebook.

The students often ask me, "What are you getting out of this whole volunteer deal?" I tell them it gives me a chance to live out a life I believe in—a life where we actually create perpetual goodness between each other. This may sound a little sappy, but the way I see it, you have to at least model that which you believe to be true.

A friend of mine once told me that he thought I was "hiding" at the shelter because I was afraid to go back out in the world due to the trauma from the collapse of my advertising agency.

Now that kinda hurt. I felt he was calling me a coward!

I assured him that I wasn't afraid of the world. The Samaritan House simply gave me the opportunity to walk my talk. Even more, writing this book gave me the chance to "talk my walk," that is, talk out loud about this walk of paying it forward so that others will do the same.

I always remind students that their charge is to live a life of paying it forward because there are a number of people who are doing that right now, for them. It's like that.

In the end, I imagine we'll always have top down, "giving back" charity programs in our system, but paying it forward is the way of the future that makes more of us responsible to each other…and to ourselves.

#2. Think this: The purpose of life is to give it away. Not that: He who dies with the most toys wins.

Whoever created this idea of dying with the most toys truly had some issues they needed to work out. So you have all the toys as you lay on your deathbed. *It's not like you can go out and play with those toys now!*

Just sayin'.

One of the chief hurdles for many of my students is their desire to get back into the world so that they, too, will accumulate more "things." Some of them have been stricken by the disease that says you only really matter when you have a lot of stuff. Unfortunately, they tie a lot of their self worth and value to this idea.

The "he who dies with the most toys wins" conventional wisdom has been driving our culture crazy for years.

As pink is the new black, giving is the new getting. Let me share with you what the experts say you get when you give. In the book *The Healing Power Of Doing Good* by researchers Luks and Payne, their years of studying volunteerism show that volunteering provides those who volunteer with a more optimistic view of life, increased energy, better perceived health, less depression, less pain, more ease in relaxing and sleeping, an improved immune system, better weight control, a healthier cardiovascular system and a speedier recovery time from surgery.

Once I started introducing this other side of the human experience and the rewards of giving life away, the students changed dramatically. It was almost like they needed permission not to go back to a life that had just punched them in the mouth and were looking for an alternative. I believe more of us would pursue giving as a way to measure our wealth if we can do more to dismantle the "he who dies with the most toys" conventional wisdom.

#3. Think this: We should honor someone every day. Not that: Don't give people too much praise or they'll get the "big head."

Many of my students had gone through some form of substance abuse.

Alcohol, crack, meth, cocaine….you name it, we had it. On any given day, ¾ of the class was recovering. Some had just emerged. Some had a few months under their belt. Others marked years on their path of sobriety. I was diligent in making sure that we gave all recovery people a round of applause. Most people don't fully appreciate the energy necessary it takes to overcome something as monstrous as an addiction. I wanted the students them to know that we as a class honor their struggle and their successes.

We do a lot of honoring in class: Recovery anniversaries. Someone's ability to tell the story of how they ended up in the shelter in the first place. Class participation. You name it. We honored the students with a round of applause. If there was ever a time I wanted the students to know that their journey was special it was as students in this class. The power of group support is very effective. Even some of the most shy in the class felt a need to participate after receiving some of the love and support. I don't want to give the illusion that it was all a love fest. We fought and argued, too. But I can truly say with great confidence that people coming from very difficult circumstances do need that acknowledgement of their accomplishment, even if that accomplishment is just waking up and not wanting to commit suicide that day. The more we honored them in their quiet victories, the more they responded. The many letters I've received over the years from former students made it clear—they were grateful for those class celebrations.

Even if it's a small thing, honor those who have done something special. The dividends can be amazing.

#4. Think this: We will end the support of homelessness in our lifetime. Not that: The poor you'll have with you always.

I consider myself expert in this subject.

Homelessness is taking one of two directions. It is either managing people who are homeless or helping them transition out of homelessness. Unfortunately, there has been an overriding conventional belief that management is the best way forward. Management is providing homeless people with warm blankets and a bowl of soup in hopes of making their homeless existence better. Religious leaders in this camp will even quote scripture to justify it: "Jesus said, the poor you'll have with you always". However, as a good minister friend of mine constantly points out, "Jesus was making an observation, based around his limited time with the Disciples. That wasn't an edict. People constantly take that scripture out of context to justify poverty and homelessness."

The worm has turned. Chances are good your city has an "End Homelessness" campaign. Chances are, it didn't exist 10 years ago. Ending homelessness is about transitioning people out of a precarious way of life instead of sending more money into the management of that life. Part of the challenge is that the management part has been heavily monetized where there is a cottage industry set up around managing *and even keeping people* in the ranks of the homeless. Grants, federal and state programs, jobs and even church, mosque and synagogue directives have been set up around helping people who are homeless *but not necessarily getting them out.* That's not to say management programs aren't needed, but without successful transition programs, homelessness will continue and probably expand. There's money involved.

I constantly hear critics say that transition is too difficult, too expensive and would require years of therapy for people in that space. My experience says none of that is true. Many societies have developed a narrative against the transition idea because we've bought the management idea hook, line and sinker, again, because there is financial incentive to keep it going.

The truth is, the new direction toward transition started when study after study found that it simply isn't cost effective to maintain homelessness. One homeless person can cost a city over $310,000 in a given year.

This new directive will not end homelessness as we know it, but it will end our *emphasis on the support of homelessness* and begin our emphasis on transitioning people. It's already happening. Programs that emphasize effective, applicable, simple approaches to transition will become gold as our conventional wisdom on this subject continues to evolve.

#5. Think this: It's good to be selfish on occasion. Not that: Selfishness is a sign of arrogance and bad form.

One of the most spectacular sights I've ever seen in my life was Hero's Plaza in Budapest, Hungary—at night. I never saw anything like it before. You have these giant, colossal stone figures, carved in elegant detail in this impressive square. The figures were all people from Hungary's history. I was moved by the Hungarian people's pride of their people, their land and their history. My Hungarian friends spoke of this place with great courage and strength.

Some people may not see it this way, but that was a form of selfishness. I was in their home and they spoke of that home with pride of ownership. If they didn't, I can assure you, there would probably not be a Hero's Plaza. This basic concept is what I wanted to communicate to my students. Without that selfishness that focused on themselves, it was impossible for them to give to their children, their loved ones and other people they claim to care for. True love for others starts with love for self. As I've constantly said in the class—you can't give what you don't have.

When the students wrote down their vision statements, I challenged them to think of themselves at their best. What would it look like if all of your challenges were met? That's the person you must be able to visualize. When you are on that path to your greatest self, you can do something for so many other people who have been waiting for you. I was always careful to say that they would be on their path and not necessarily at their destination. We don't have to wait for all of our challenges to be met before we can pay forward goodness.

I reminded my students if there ever was a time to be selfish, it has to be now, in the middle of their most difficult time.

In the long run I believe all of us will benefit from this form of selfishness.

Do Some New Stuff To Change Up Your Thought Pattern.

All of us could use a little help when it comes to shaking up our conventional wisdom. Here are some tools I've discovered along with way while working with people in transition, leadership groups and NGOs around the world:

1. Have coffee with a liar. I think we undervalue liars in our society. Of course, they go against our moral concepts of integrity, but as long as you know they're lying, they can provide some of the most insightful views of the human condition. Besides that, chances are you'll see some of yourself in the things they say. Notice I said coffee instead of breakfast, lunch or dinner. You don't want to hang out too long with a liar, lest you pick up some of their habits.

2. Quit watching television for a three-month period of time. I made this suggestion in my first book several years ago. I stand by the statement that it breaks the hold pop culture has on your life.

3. Have lunch with an elder. It's come to my attention that our elders may or may not necessarily have wisdom, *but they do have a lot of experience.* Their experiences can provide a very cool context for our life journeys that will help us get the wisdom we need. Remember, wisdom is our ability to interpret those experiences effectively for ourselves. My grandmother provides me with insight as she talks about everything from scripture to her favorite recipe to the weather. I get several generations worth of knowledge in one setting. How cool is that? All she asks in return is that I bring her a glass of room-temperature water.

4. Get beyond the light pollution of the city and check out the Milky Way. My first night in Africa, I went way out to an open field to drink in the actual experience of having my feet on the Motherland. I looked up and saw the gorgeous Milky Way and realized we were part of a larger community of stars. Several students told me that it put life on earth in perspective, and made them want to dig deeper for their life's purpose. You may not have a poetic life-changing moment, but it can be quite soothing some night when things are a bit tough in your world.

5. Become a babysitter. I'm lucky to have a good friend who has three wonderful daughters, two of whom are five-

and six-years old at this writing. Even though I have two grown sons of my own, the joy I get from seeing these young girls is beyond words. Watching them go through the emotions of joy, sorrow, frustration, anger and glee in the span of 4 minutes reminds me of the beauty of the human experience and how each moment is not like the one before. Spending time savoring their "beingness" as well as their honesty is clarifying. Even if you have children, spend some time with someone else's. Keep plenty of candy and money in case you need to engage in delicate negotiations.

6. Google something to death. Take one subject and just follow it until you can't follow it anymore. It's a simple thing, but it takes you to places you would not otherwise go. This leads to expanded capacity.

Inspiration

#6. Think this: There is no box. Not that: Think outside the box.

If ever there was a corporate catch phrase for our times it was "think outside the box." In every meeting or workshop, some guy or gal in a suit would stand in front of the group and say something about how we need to think differently about the company or the organization. We need to "think outside the box." Little did they know, but every time they would use the box as a reference point, they put us in another box. In my years of teaching empowerment at homeless shelters, I realized the first thing I needed to tell my students was that there is no box. That means, there is no reference point that tied them down to the lifestyle they feel had enslaved them. This level of freedom allowed people to soar in their imaginations about what was now possible for their lives going forward. Without a box as a checkpoint, they were free to explore areas they were sure were off limits to them. It certainly opened them up to newer, deeper ideas than they would have explored otherwise.

My speculation after working with both the desperately poor and the amazingly well-off is that the box provides a kind of safety blanket to reality. In a world of uncertainty, we can always count on the tried and tested, for better or worse, to lead us back to a place of familiarity. Psychologist and researcher Dr. David Hawkins in his book, *I: Reality and Subjectivity*, says familiarity is a function of the ego. The ego doesn't like to have its world view challenged or brought into question. It may feel threatened by contrary information and become defensive because it is being made to look "wrong." Using the box as a tether is a kind of a Dwayne Wade "head fake" for the ego. It seems like it's going left into something different but really it's going right and resuming that old path again.

"There is no box" is the next step in the process of redefining the world for people who have lived beneath their abilities.

#7. Think this: Life is harder when you're ignorant. Not that: Ignorance is bliss.

My emphasis in teaching this class was how ignorance was the number one tool in keeping the students cycling around in a world of homelessness and poverty. I made a strong effort to get the students to recognize how their avoidance of basic knowledge was making life disproportionately harder for them. Knowing the options they have, being aware of how the legal system worked and identifying help sources through a simple internet search became part of the course. I brought the point home to them about how rampant ignorance is in our society by sharing with them parts of an interview I saw on YouTube where a British film crew talked to a variety of Americans in different cities. These are some of the questions and some of the answers:

Q. "What month did the tragedy of 9/11 take place?"

"Uh, August?"

"I think it was in October."

"Ah, October 2004, and I was even in New York then."

Q. "Name a country whose name starts with U."

"Yugoslavia"

"Utah"

"Utopia"

Q. "What's the religion of Israel?"

"Israeli"

"Islam"

"Catholic, probably"

Q. "What's the religion of Buddhist Monks?"

"Islamic, I don't know."

Q. "Who won the Vietnam War?"

"We did….wait, were we even in the Vietnam war?"

Q. "Who is Fidel Castro?"

"A singer?"

Q. "How many sides does a triangle have?"

"Damn…..four"

"There are no sides.....one?"

Q. "What's the currency used in the United Kingdom?"

"Queen Elizabeth money?"

"Possibly American money."

Q. "What countries did former President Bush name as being part of the Axis of Evil?"
"New York, California...."

"Jerusalem"

"I know Germany's one of them."

"Florida".

Q. "What state does KFC come from?"

"I don't know. I really don't know."

Folks, you can't make this stuff up. This kind of ignorance is more comatose than blissful.

Maybe the "ignorance is bliss" conventional wisdom worked at some point in time in the history of the world, but my suspicion is that most who practiced it were also the people who suffered under it. Just my guess.

I never really got lofty or romantic when I was telling the students about the importance of knowledge when it comes to freedom. I just spoke about it in relation to their basic, everyday needs. Life is harder when you're ignorant.

#8. Think this: Go for it on fourth down. Not that: Kick it.

You can't teach courage. But you can make it more accessible. That was one of the most important things I've learned about working with people walking through transition. As much as we'd like to teach or even give people courage, that's something they have to find in themselves. With my students, I decided to break courage down in terms of sports, namely football and the infamous fourth down decision.

Anyone who watches American-style football with any regularity knows that teams often punt the ball or kick a field goal on fourth down. The conventional wisdom is that you play to not lose the game by tying it with a field goal or you punt the ball so far away, the other team has less of a chance of scoring, thus increasing the odds that your team will win. According to an emerging number of statisticians and economists, going for a first down or touchdown instead of kicking the ball is a better bet. One guy from this new school of thought is David Berri, a sports economist and professor of applied economics at Southern Utah University,

He comes flat out and says teams punt much more frequently than they should. "You don't want to punt when you have the ball in the area of your opponent's 30- to 40-yard line," he says. "The cost-benefit study indicates you should go for it. If you punt, they're probably going to get the ball on the 20 anyway, which isn't much of a gain, and it's a long field goal. The value of going for it increases dramatically in that area of the field."

I started talking to the students with these facts just to let them know that the odds are often in their favor when they decide to take chances where contemporary conventional wisdom tells them to play it safe. We started describing fourth-down scenarios in their lives where they were asked to either go for it or punt. Most of the time (not all), we realized that when they punted (using the analogy) the situation didn't get better. In many cases, it got worse. Going for it on fourth down is not necessarily the best idea all of the time, but making it part of the discussion instead of going for the punt immediately increased the student's courage ratio and possibilities for success. The numbers bear it out. Go for it.

#9. Think this: Call it the empowerment movement. Not that: Call it the self-help recovery movement.

Life is tough. Your parents had their own problems. Things won't go right sometimes. You're a victim. Think positive.

There, I just saved you $20. You won't have to go out and buy the latest self-help recovery book on the stands. I just summed up what most of them are saying.

I'm being a bit facetious, but there is a backlash happening now against the so-called self-help recovery movement. This is the movement that pretty much calls you a victim, looks for someone to blame for your challenges, and focuses the rest of your life on the healing process. Some people are throwing Oprah Winfrey under the bus in this backlash, but Oprah simply stepped out in front of a parade that was in full effect. It is almost vogue for Westerners to find something to hate, and some of the self-help recovery authors, speakers and seminar leaders are giving these haters red meat.

This is a very sensitive subject for a lot of my students because many of them are looking for support for their journey through transition. Many of them started reading some these books to find that magic bullet that would end their problems.

The only problem is that the magic bullet they're looking for doesn't exist.

Some of my students have told me how they followed some of those self-help recovery gurus to the "T," and still were having the same experience they had before. That's when I started introducing The Window Effect Method. Because so many of my students were the broken victims of religious and new thought formulas that didn't eventually work for them. I wanted to make sure they had tools that didn't over promise.

The Window Effect Method emphasizes 5 core ideas:

1. Windows of opportunity show up in our lives all the time if we look for them.

2. They are not guarantees of success, but opportunities.

3. Challenges are part of the human experience.

4. When you experience good, pay it forward.

5. We are all connected.

You cannot come to this population—who have been through crazy stuff—with false hope. You have to have wide-eyed, practical real-world vision with great inspiration.

The result of using this approach? An empowerment approach that accounts for disappointment and unfortunate events as well as hope, possibilities and probabilities, community connectedness, volunteerism and personal transformation.

So the next time you feel an urge to find a guru to help you discover your inner child, your shame self or your victimized life, resist the temptation and go volunteer somewhere. It'll give you context and show you the way to empowerment.

#10. Think this: *Ubuntu*—We are all connected. Not that: I'm all about rugged individualism.

My many stays in South Africa exposed me to the concept of Ubuntu. This foundational African philosophical concept is a spiritual and humanist philosophy focusing on people's allegiances and relations with each other. The word has its origin in the Bantu languages of southern Africa. *Ubuntu* is one of the premier classical African concepts. When I first heard it, it resonated immediately. Ubuntu basically means we are individuals who are connected and dependent on each other. We are group, but this group is made up of individuals and each individual must be respected. It is a perfect definition of interdependence.

My South African family helped me understand this concept on an intimate basis. I looked for Ubuntu in everything, everywhere, all the time. This searching led me to issue a definitive statement:

Show me where there is evil in the world, and I'll show you someone who does not believe in Ubuntu.

Think about it. From Stalin, to Hitler, to Pol Pot, to the Rape of Nanking, to slavery in America, someone, somewhere came to the conclusion that they were not connected to "those other people;" therefore, they can do things to others they would never do to someone they are connected with. The denial of Ubuntu is the root of all evil.

Contrary to the myth that homeless people are stuck in the "dependency on the system" idea, most of my students would come in to the shelter with some concept of rugged individualism—you know, "I'm a self made person", "I have to pull myself up by my bootstraps", "I don't really need this assistance." That idea often got in the way of their getting the help and services they needed to pull themselves up. I had to convince them that accepting help doesn't take away from their individuality or their integrity as stand-up people. It only means part of being a powerful person is seeing yourself as part of the collective. We are only as strong individually as we are collectively. That is the essence of Ubuntu.

Where my students run into problems is that they don't understand the most successful of us depended on other people to get us to where we are. We may run that rugged individual rap for the sake of impressing people, but we had help—lots of it—from our connections. I started teaching the students the power of networking and changing up their social circles. Understanding connections is understanding Ubuntu.

Coming from an advertising background, I know the power of myth making. Myths can die long, hard deaths because of one reason: no one has to come up with the facts to back them up. Thus, they exist as a kind of social ghost—never proven, but never having to be proved, either. Kind of like "God helps those who helps themselves." It's not Scripture, but people will swear it is. Such is also the case of "rugged individualism." To bring my point home in my class, I went to the latest science to help dismantle this social ghost.

Physicist Nicolas Gisin sent entangled particles zooming along optical fibers until they were seven miles apart. But whatever action they took, the communication between them happened instantaneously. No self-respecting physicist today doubts the connectedness between bits of light or matter, or even entire clusters of atoms. They're intimately linked in a manner suggesting there's no space between them, and no time influencing their behavior. This is the very essence of our being. We are connected on a sub-atomic level. Our job is to recognize and leverage this truth.

In some ways, the reality of our connectedness is being born out in the social mediums of Facebook, Twitter and MySpace. The ancient African philosophy of Ubuntu is now taking center stage because of its core statement:

I am because we are—we are because I am.

The African philosophy of Ubuntu creates a working person's understanding of a greater scientific truth that we are only now discovering. It's possible that our acceptance of this idea will direct us into ways we can leverage it to the advantage of more people.

#11. Think this: What we believe will determine what it will be. Not that: That which doesn't kill you, makes you stronger.

When I was younger, I was told that wisdom comes with age. The longer I lived, I started to realize that is simply not a guarantee. I know plenty of old fools. The same is true about trial by fire. Working with homeless people made it abundantly clear to me that which doesn't kill you doesn't necessarily make you stronger. That statement originated with Nietzsche and my experience says he missed the mark. In fact, Nietzsche faced his own challenges along the road. Those challenges didn't kill him, but he did eventually die insane. The truth is, that which doesn't kill you can make you weaker and more vulnerable.

What I have discovered along the way is what people believe about what they experience will eventually determine if it becomes something that can strengthen their life's journey or make it more challenging. In my classes, I have often quoted the Observer Effect as a scientific foundation: the observed is affected by the observer.

To illustrate this idea, I draw a circle on the board. I ask the class what it is. Out of 50 people, I'll get 15 to 20 different answers, from a pizza to a zero to a hole to the Sun and so on. How can there be so many different interpretations of the same thing? Simple—our life experiences and beliefs will give us an interpretation that is unique to each of us.

Two people are involved in a car accident. One person says it was the worst experience of her life. Another says it was a doorway that opened up life for him. For one person, it was an experience that didn't make her stronger, but more sad, depressed and despondent. For the other, it's a new lease. That which doesn't kill us does not guarantee that we will become stronger. We would have to choose strength over desperateness.

I always admired how many Continental Africans thought about death. Their perspective made death not the fearful monster that we don't talk about here in the West. They seemed to take the bite out of it by their casualness toward it. I was in the Kalahari Desert near the Botswana border recently to do some research on a film I was helping to produce. It was 4 in the afternoon and my driver and my interpreter told me we needed to leave to get back into town now since we were at least 4 hours away. I told them I needed just a little more time to get more information. They both smiled at each other, then smiled at me. I asked, "What's up?" My interpreter said in a calm, peaceful voice: "We could stay a little longer, but we run the risk of being trampled to death by black elephants, killed by hordes of Kudu or mauled by wild boar." I laughed because I thought they just wanted to get back to civilization. They smiled, took out a press clipping about four people who were killed the previous week when black elephants trampled their truck.

My reply: "What are we all standing around for? Let's get the hell out of here!"

My driver and interpreter made death real, but not beyond us. The more I thought about it, the more their belief helped me start to pay attention to my long-held ideas about something that is as natural as birth.

The key to navigating through challenging times is not to put ourselves in harm's way, thinking that this will make us stronger, but to proactively turn each event into a conscious tool that can help avoid crazy situations in the future.

I won't be driving through the Kalahari at night anytime soon.

#12. Think this: Happiness leads to success. Not that: Success leads to happiness.

I would regularly hammer into my students that being happy will lead to their success as opposed to waiting for personal success to arrive, then they would become happy. "Chet, how am I going to be happy right now. I'm homeless!" Fair enough. What I directed them to do was to find elements of happiness in their lives and build a meditation around that happiness. The reason why this was introduced to the students is because all of the research out there says that creating that happiness will increase the odds of their success.

A 2005 review of 225 studies in the *Psychological Bulletin*, published by the American Psychological Association, has found that cheerful people are more likely to try new things and challenge themselves, which reinforces positive emotion and leads to success in work, good relationships and strong health.

The research suggests that happy individuals are predisposed to seek out and undertake new goals in life and this reinforces positive emotions. What's more, chronically happy people are in general more successful across many life domains than less happy people and their happiness is in large part a consequence of their positive emotions rather than vice versa.

Great, Chet. So how do we become happy if we're sad? Maybe it's as simple as getting older.

Dr. Arthur Stone of Stony Brook University gathered data about happiness from 340,000 people. His conclusion? Eventually, we become happier in life as we get older, particularly after age 50. The reason? Our focus is about the smaller things—relationships, good food, decent health. The other things that kept us on the treadmill—achievement, possessions and status—no longer have the same influence in our lives as we age. This particular path to happiness is in keeping with Buddhist philosophy that says the source of all suffering is our attachment to things and outcomes. As life goes on, those things and outcomes simply don't matter as much. Unfortunately, most of us don't get that lesson until we're further up in age. However, this information may provide us with some insight if we find that happiness frequently escapes us.

Before you spend a lot of your money and time buying the books and tapes of happiness and self empowerment experts, you might want to take the first step in the process and release your attachment to things and outcomes. Not an easy task in a society that usually measures personal worth on what you do and what you've got, but it may prove to be a quite effective in the long haul.

#13. Think this: The key to a better life is having expanded capacity. Not that: The key to a better life is having a positive mental attitude.

In 2006, the world was all abuzz about a book, then later the movie called *The Secret.* This book claimed an ancient secret had the recipe for all of the world's challenges and ills, and even suggested that if you think hard enough, you, too, like Elmer J. Fudd, could become an millionaire as well could own a mansion and a yacht.

If all of this sounds vaguely familiar to some of you, it's because the same claim has been made generation after generation through the conventional wisdom called Positive Mental Attitude. Its latest incarnation has been in *The Secret* by its New Thought supporters. But it has also shown up in North American Evangelical circles as "Name It and Claim It" prosperity theology.

The entire premise is that somehow you could think, pray or believe your way to riches untold. It works—but primarily for the motivational speakers and preachers who deliver this gospel to you. However, the dark side of this conventional wisdom is that it puts millions of people at financial risk around the world and has a casual disregard for sound health and financial judgment. Journalist Hanna Rosin argues that the millions of subscribers to prosperity gospel through positive mental attitude may have "pumped air into the housing bubble" that caused the current financial crisis, by ignoring "the dull stuff of hourly wages and bank account statements"... and the prudent calculation of what spending can be afforded, in favor of "financial miracles."

Many of my students ended up at the shelter under this belief system. I usually ended up with the people who the PMA people don't talk about—the ones that did believe and did all the right stuff according to their formula, but things still didn't work out for them.

To be fair, the PMA people have it partly right. It is true that whatever you focus on has a tendency of showing up in your life. Based on my years of working with people in the most desperate of situations, I've found out that it's because negative people simply seek the same people, places and situations that validate their experience to date. In other words, if you're cycling in poverty and have no social contacts outside of other poverty-stricken people, chances are good you will maintain your socioeconomic status, which validates your belief about your existence. You are simply reinforcing it through your social contacts and environment. Effective ways of breaking the cycle can come through some dramatic or traumatic event that will create an opportunity to step out of the familiar, like winning the lottery, gaining a significant inheritance, or going through a life-changing near-death experience. Since human beings seek continuity and are creatures of habit, these kinds of cycle-breaking events are usually forced on us through something unforeseen.

As always, there are exceptions to the rule. But as a number of social scientists are now realizing, expanding capacity presents the greatest opportunity for us to create a more sustainable world of new possibilities.

The "expanded capacity" idea means that you are not waiting for a dramatic or traumatic event to force you into a new life, but are intentionally creating it by expanding the database of knowledge you currently have. I would say this key concept instantly changed the lives of many of my students. It didn't require hype or hoopla, just a patient and diligent introduction of a new concept or idea at least once a week. I was able to provide that through the class.

From superstring theory to anthropology to the future of society to sexual cues between men and women, I kept expanding their experience with the presumption that this would lead to an increased desire to step outside of their current social cycle. This approach was directly cited by the students in their exit interviews as the reason why they were able to do more and see more.

If you want to search for a "secret" way to a better life, you can. But I've found that the tools of expanded capacity are no secret and can be more effective than anything else out there.

#14. Think this: Think proactively. Not that: If it ain't broke, don't fix it.

A friend of mine gave me a great quote the other day. He said, "Mediocrity is the only place where people can actualize their full potential." I don't know if that's his original quote or whether he borrowed it from some other place, but it's a gem. "If it ain't broke, don't fix it" is the gospel of the mediocre. The implication is that action is generally to be avoided, that the status quo is probably just fine, and that you should wait for a true crisis before intervening.

My guess is that every DMV office in the world has the "If it ain't broke..." quote hanging on their walls.

The challenge my students faced was that they were not used to being proactive. Most of their lives were based around being reactive to their environment and what other people were going to do to them. From some of the students' perspective, things were already broke. Why try to fix it? To counter this, we introduced an exercise called "In the best of all worlds, I would...." From there, they would name one thing they would do proactively in their lives. Of course, I would then ask them, "What's stopping you from doing that?" It was a start in the process of breaking them out of the "if it ain't broke" conventional wisdom.

Things break down. To suggest somehow if we just don't seek to improve something it will never break down defies logic, but the "if it ain't broke" conventional wisdom phrase has been with us for eons. This particular conventional wisdom is probably responsible for less being done in the world than worker's strikes. It is changing, however, with the new movements in health, business management and education. People are recognizing that it is much more cost effective to develop something on top of the base that's already established than to start from scratch after the system broke down due to lack of courage in trying something new.

There are definite benefits to being brave and thinking ahead.

#15. Think this: Opportunity is always knocking. Not that: Opportunity only knocks once.

The idea behind the old "knocks once" theory is that you need to jump on it when it first appears because chances are it won't happen again.

I don't know about you, but there seems to be an element of desperation at the heart of that wise old saying. My experience has been where there's desperation, there's trouble.

Working with thousands of homeless people over the years has also led me to understand this: opportunity never knocks once. It knocks all the time. It just shows up differently from time to time. Sure, it may not seem recognizable initially because we're focused on a particular way of how it should show up. But once you get past that, you start to see the opportunity or opportunities everywhere.

You would be amazed at how so many of my student's lives were changed simply when we expanded their definition of opportunity. They would often say, "I would see that all the time but never saw it as an opportunity!" It's very similar to when you first purchase a new car, let's say a 2010 Mustang. All of the sudden, you start seeing Mustangs everywhere. It seems as though everyone went out and got a Mustang simply because you bought one. The truth is, the other Mustangs were always there, you just didn't see them until your perspective changed. The Mustangs moved from invisible to visible.

Opportunity is always knocking, you just have to listen for the knock.

#16. Think this: I have a personal vision statement. Not that: I have a five-year plan.

I'm actually a big fan of five-year plans, but my observation is that very few people actually follow their five-year plan through. It's not that they aren't committed. It's just that our life terrain changes so much in five months, let alone five years, that we end up scrapping or changing that plan anyway. I truly do believe in plans, but let me provide a way we can maintain the elemental source of the five-year plan no matter how it changes: the personal vision statement.

Of all the things I've implemented in the class, nothing was more powerful than this particular tool. The personal vision statement is not reciting our assets against our liabilities or a recitation of our educational accomplishments. Rather, it that states who you are, whether it's true right now or not. Some samples we used in the class included:

"I am healthy."

"I have more peace."

"I make good decisions."

"My financial world is stable and prosperous."

We would have the student repeat this simple statement once before they go to bed at night and once when they got up in the morning for 28 days.

What the vision statement does is make sure you understand why you're doing the 5-year plan. Once the vision is established, the plan is simply changeable tactics to achieve the vision. The goal remains the same. The roads to get there may, and probably will, change.

There is no *hocus pocus* in this practice, but it does do five things for sure:

1. Helps the student visualize beyond their current difficult circumstances to find hope going forward.

2. Provides the student with a structured tool to counter some of the negative information they may receive on an ongoing basis.

3. Helps the student establish a new habit that is affirming and uplifting.

4. Increases the student's odds of being able to achieve the goal of this vision statement.

5. Helps the student become comfortable with a discipline as part of their new life.

As any person who has obtained goals will tell you, it really is work. What empowers the person to do the work is to visualize the goal through a constant, continuous affirmation statement. I would submit that without a powerful, compelling, yet simple vision statement, it is virtually impossible, save winning the lottery, to achieve even minimal goals. The amount of work involved without a vision is simply too exhausting. Inspiration with a powerful idea can help people get through the most difficult of challenges.

I knew the students needed that boost, so my job was not only to keep them focused on the discipline of their late-night and early-morning vision statement recitals, but to help paint the details of a better world on the other side of their climb.

Never doubt the power of inspiration through the vision statement.

#17. Think this: People respond best to inspiration. Not that: People respond best to motivation.

The two are not the same.

Motivation is the activation of goal-oriented behavior. Action is taken to reach a specific goal. Motivational speakers provide a path where you can achieve a certain goal. Religious leaders give you a plan so that you will eventually end up in heaven or some form of eternal bliss. Your boss rewards you with a raise once you accomplish a specific task, thus, your motivation is the raise.

This seems like pretty straightforward stuff. You tell people do this and they'll get that. They should walk right into goal-oriented behavior, right?

Apparently, motivation is not enough. Workers fail to achieve the task they were set to do, motivational speakers fail to get people past their current situation, and religious organizations are constantly worried about "backsliders."

When I was a teenager, I was a band geek. I played a French horn, I was in the concert band and the marching band as well as orchestra. I couldn't buy a date.

Then I discovered the "fast" girls. These were the girls who wore more makeup than the church girls, put on shorter dresses and smacked gum real loud. I was always fascinated by them but was told by my church-going friends that I would go to hell in a hand basket if I fooled around with those girls. I often fantasized about them, but I couldn't see myself with them, until one of those fast girls actually told a friend of mine that she liked me and wanted to date me.

Me, a certified geek.

I developed an entire vision around me being with a fast girl, stimulated by that one statement. It seemed as though my vision of the world expanded beyond everything I knew when I realized one of the prized Jezebels from down the road thought I was cute. I then developed a new vision of myself and the world, simply because I was dating a fast girl. Even the threat of going to hell couldn't keep me from pursuing this emotional and revealing change in my life. It became clear to me that the human spirit takes courage to new heights when it has a bigger vision of its existence beyond what it sees. This is what is called inspiration. Giving us rewards for accomplishing a task is kinda good, but helping us see a greater vision via inspiration is much better.

This was our working definition of inspiration for the class:

Inspiration is receiving a new vision above and beyond that which you see in front of you and having the courage to pursue it even in the face of potential danger or failure.

Because of the high recidivism rate among homeless people, it became clear to me that the best way to help reduce those numbers is not to use the carrot or the stick to motivate, but to connect a new vision that could lay the foundation for a bigger vision of their lives.

If motivation was the answer, most of our problems would be solved. Inspiration provides a more powerful view of something that once seemed beyond us.

Even things like fast girls.

#18. Think this: Success requires you to work smarter. Not that: Success requires you to work harder.

The one theme I definitely got from my mother and father was the power of working hard. They gave me and my siblings a work ethic second to none. They didn't have to pound it into us. They just lived it. Once I was in college, I knew I had become my parents. I worked at three radio stations, a fast food restaurant and the Student Center cafeteria, all at the same time just to pay for my college education. That path to working hard paid off eventually when my advertising agency became a success beyond my imagination. Working harder is a good thing, but many of my students were working hard. Why weren't their efforts bearing the fruits that my efforts did back in the day?

The new world we live in is asking for something different from us. It supports the success of our physical efforts, but to achieve full success, we have to work smarter.

If you spend time with the most contemporary successful people, you'll see the work hard part got them to one level, but the work smart part made their success sustainable in the long run. How do you know if you're working smarter? Here are some key questions:

1. **Do you have a life outside of your work?** Working smarter people know that making social connections in social and play settings outside of work can lead to greater success.

2. **Do you give your mind time to rejuvenate?** Working smarter people recognize that when a point of diminishing return sets in, it's time to take a break and go do some life stuff. Most great ideas tend to occur outside of the laboratory or work setting when doing life stuff.

3. **Do you give time to your support system?** No one operates in a vacuum. A healthy support system allows us to think through decisions and help us out when things go south. Making sure they are supported makes sure you are supported.

As I became stuck trying to work out a bunch of ideas

around this book, a good friend of mine suggested I take up Salsa. I asked, "To what end?" He said, "You need playtime to get unstuck." Sure enough, the more I danced, the clearer my ideas became. Great ideas came to me, right there on the dance floor between a cumbia move and a cross body lead.

Working hard is good. Working smart is better.

#19. Think this: People change all the time. Not that: You can't teach an old dog new tricks.

Many people don't believe in change. That is especially true of many of my students. When talking about their experience, I'd often hear someone saying. "Well, this is just who I am." Once they agreed to that, the field of opportunity immediately shrunk to only a few choices. Once they said that, I would ask them one pretty basic question: Are you the same person now than you were when you were 10-years old? 20-years old? Of course they would say no. Their beliefs have changed because they have had new experiences. Their friends have probably changed over the years, too. If they had a life-changing event (as many of them have), chances are they might have changed their spiritual views. And if they've had children, they've probably modified their priorities.

They've changed. I bet you have, too.

As much as people like to cite that old conventional wisdom of not being able to teach old dogs new tricks, the truth is people change and learn "new tricks" all the time.

My experience working with people in transition is that people do change, but the real question is can people transform? Transformation is where we intend a direction for our lives. The change we experience is usually by default. Transformation is by design. This too is available to everyone, but it does require a level of work and commitment.

So the conventional wisdom of not being able to teach an old dog new tricks doesn't hold water simply because people can and do learn and implement new things all the time by simply being human and accumulating experiences. Transformation means directing our human experiences to create a chosen way forward, and choosing to learn new tricks.

#20. Think this: We learn more from our success than our failures. Not that: We learn more from our failures than our success.

Yeah, it is true there are a few things we can gather from our bad experiences. I always emphasize to the students the importance of not letting a teachable moment get away from us. But the tide has turned where it seems as though we believe wisdom only comes from bad times. I'm here to say, that is patently not true. There is a whole lot of learning that comes from remembering and reemphasizing the things we've done right.

A new study done on monkeys at MIT's Picower Institute For Learning and Memory suggests that the brain neurons involved in learning may process information more effectively after a success than after a failure, which in turn leads to an improvement in behavior. The researchers noted in the test that the monkey's neurons actually became more "finely tuned" after a correct response than after an incorrect response, meaning that the neurons were able to better distinguish between the two different associations that the monkey was learning.

While it is true we can get some learning from our mistakes, this study would indicate that the more we experience success, the better we learn about how to be more successful.

Failure can be a harsh taskmaster, but not necessarily a good teacher. The debunking of this conventional wisdom actually gives more credence to another conventional wisdom saying: nothing breeds success like success.

#21. Think this: Change your thoughts, change your stress. Not that: Life is stressful.

Along with the conventional wisdom that life is tough is its sister statement that life is stressful. Well, yeah, it is. Welcome to the human experience. But just because it's stressful doesn't mean it's not manageable. My job was to teach my students those management skills. That's when we started teaching meditation practices in the classrooms. It's a great stress management tool when quieting the mind and putting your thoughts in check.

It's all about the thoughts.

Psychologist Dr. Andrew Bernstein, author of *The Myth Of Stress*, says this: "Stress comes from your thoughts about your circumstances, not the circumstances themselves. More specifically, stress is produced as a result of a certain kind of abstract thought—counterfactual thought. Whenever we think this way, we experience stress." He goes on to give examples of this kind of thought: "I should weigh less" , "I should be more successful" , "My boss shouldn't micromanage me." The more counterfactual thoughts we have, the more stress we experience, he concludes.

In my class, I teach people how to identify these thoughts, then challenge them so that they think differently, and as a result feel different and can act differently. But it starts with deep change in perspective.

His conversation is shaking up the medical profession, but it stands to reason that there is a mind/body connection. The students started to appreciate this connection and started getting into the meditation.

#22. Think this: Humankind is transitioning. Not that: It's the end of the world.

If there is a group of people who can truly talk with expert precision about the end of the world, it would be homeless people. While many of us may be waiting for the Antichrist, the return of Jesus or the 12th Imam or maybe even the aliens to come and scoop us up, homeless people have already gone through the process of having their world completely dismantled. Walking with them through this period of time brought me to three conclusions:

1. We focus on the end instead of the beginning.
2. We see change as the enemy.
3. We don't understand transition.

The beginning of something is just as valid and as real as the end of something, but our cultural emphasis leans toward the end. We have political movements that demonize change and are constantly telling people we need to go back to the way things were. And notice how little time we really give toward understanding transition. That's probably because transition is a time of uncertainty. People don't like that.

I'll admit, at one time in my life I was like that old dude on the Hitchcock movie, *The Birds*. I was always going around saying, "It's the end of the world." First, I based that on my Christian upbringing and the end-time prophecies in

Revelations. Then, as I got older, I created my own set of prophecies that must first manifest to indicate the end of the world is at hand. They are:

- The Cubs win the World Series.
- Pluto will be restored to its planet status.
- Soccer (football) will become the number one sport in the US.
- Everyone will agree that butterscotch pecan ice cream is the only ice cream that counts!
- It will be verified that Tupac really is dead.
- Carly Simon will finally reveal who she's referring to in her song "You're So Vain."

When all of these things happen, I think we can all max out our credit cards and head to that bunker in Idaho. The world is coming to an end.

While none of us really knows what humankind's next transition will look like or when it will come, it is clear that the conventional wisdom of the end of the world being near is as old as humankind itself. Since the beginning of our existence, there was some person with a sign talking about the end being near. If near is over hundreds of thousands of years, then yes...that person was right.

At every major societal transition, there were people predicting the end of the world. From the Romans seeing it after the Visigoths climbed over the gates, to Africans seeing it during Colonization, to Europeans seeing it during the Dark Ages, to Chinese seeing it during The Rape of Nanking, everyone saw the end of our existence at one time or another.

The emerging science is to see it as transition. We are becoming something different than what we are and to the casual observer, it looks like dread.

That dread is often translated to our predictions of the future. The New World Order dictatorship is what most doom sayers are predicting as they track the end times. Perhaps this is also a time to advance another scenario, one that says we'll become a more enlightened, more plural world.

So while our current state of affairs may be toppled, a new version of life on earth may be emerging. That's not necessarily a bad thing. If you are a victim of genocide in Darfur, you'd probably agree with me.

Change is the one constant throughout the universe. I say we go with it.

#23. Think this: Life is messy. Not that: I should go to college, get a high paying job, buy the nice home, get the expensive imported car, get the gold watch and retire.

We should have picked up the clue at birth. Mothers and the babies are near death during the entire ordeal. There's a lot of blood, pain (some more than others) and crying. Life is messy from the start.

So many of my students could not figure out why their lives were so messy. They would look around and say, "Why is my life so messy and so many other people seemed to have gotten it together?" I reminded them not to be fooled by appearances and not to buy into the conventional wisdom of how life is supposed to go.

Most of us have lived enough life to know that neat life narratives simply don't apply to the real world. The challenge is that many people build their personal goals around this archaic conventional wisdom, even though our actual experience is saying something else is going on. When the two don't match, you have disappointment.

From divorce to cancer to winning the lottery to unexpected births, to hirings, firings and layoffs, life is simply not very neat. Our ability to appreciate this reality may help us reconcile a lot of questions about why things are don't always go "right." Since the 70s, tons of books talk about our messy existence. They include Harold Kushner's *When Bad Things Happen To Good People*, Tinker Melvin's *Why Do Bad Things Happen To Good People*, Philip Yancey's *Where Is God When It Hurts* and Therese Rado's *How To Go On Living When Someone You Love Dies*.

If your bathroom has bathtub ring, spots on the mirror, shower scum and a dirty toilet bowl, don't fret. Those stains are usually part of a well-used bathroom. You don't take a wrecking ball to the bathroom. You just find products to help clean it up—not once, but pretty regularly. Consider your life messiness part of a well-used life. Consider ongoing cleaning just a part of the deal.

#24. Think this: God looks like all of us. Not that: God is an old white man with a beard, sitting on a cloud.

They say never talk about religion and/or politics in mixed company, but that's exactly what I did in my class with the students. During one of our classes when we were doing some visioning of what our future looked like, I noticed one student scribbling a picture of an old man on a cloud with a bolt of lighting in one hand, preparing his aim on someone he was watching down below. This god looked mean, aggressive and constipated. I asked the student, "Is this how you see God?" He laughed and said, "Well, yeah kinda." We may not think about it, but popular media has established a very familiar God caricature that has set up shop in our collective subconscious. The problem we face is that is that we really don't know what God looks like. Of course, if you don't believe in God, you don't have this problem. But for believers, having the God of all things painted in a certain way has political and personal cost.

When Charlemagne came to power in 800 as the Holy Roman Emperor, iconoclasm was the rule of the day. In Christianity, iconoclasm has generally been a literal interpretation of the Ten Commandments, which forbid the making and worshipping of "graven images" thus, no pictures. However, Charlemagne started a campaign to end this practice so that the Christian God could be seen and imaged. From that time on through the European Middle Ages and through the Renaissance, God started showing up in the likeness and image of the people who were painting him. You can imagine that to a French, German or Italian painter, God would look European, which makes sense. However, with the spread of Western ideas in the world, so went the spread of a de facto European orthodoxy of what God looks like to everybody else.

In a highly animated discussion I conducted in one of my classes at the homeless shelter, one of my clients asked me, "What do you think God looks like?" I replied, "That guy I see in the mirror every morning, because if I can't see the creator of all things in me, I'm in deep trouble."

Fortunately, Hollywood is also seeing God through the eyes of all of us through several very on-point interpretations in the movies by entertainers Morgan Freeman, Alanis Morissette, and Jose Perez.

When I started emphasizing a more multicultural version of The Maker Of All Things, many of my students started changing their vision from a God that was vengeful task master to a personal friend. For whatever reason, when the class collectively started re-imaging God in the image of all people, they started talking about God in a much more friendly, affable and cooler way.

If your world is full of mean people, mean situations and mean possibilities, it might have something to do with that mean guy you call God. Check it out.

#25. Think this: Live a life of non-attachment. Not that: That non-attachment life stuff is Eastern religion mumbo jumbo.

Yeah, some of this does come from a Buddhist friend of mine who basically told me that one of the streams of thought in Buddhism was that a devotee should not be attached to things. I thought that was interesting, but we made up our own version of the non-attachment in the class.

The basic challenge homeless people face is the loss of their things—homes, cars, personal possessions. I reminded them of how things come and go all the time.

I can testify to that idea personally.

So I proposed that the true essence of non-attachment was not being attached to outcome. When we are not attached to a particular way of how things should go, we open up more possibilities. Instead of one particular outcome, hundreds of other possibilities now are available to us, simply because we don't limit ourselves to one. We are no longer "attached" to the outcome. That to me seems to be a more reasonable interpretation of a life of non-attachment. It certainly went over well with the students. They saw this as a way of opening up to possibilities they never thought about before because they were so locked in on one kind of outcome.

Who says living a life of non-attachment was a hard thing?

#26. Think this: All things are possible. Not that: You can't have everything.

When I tell people that I teach my students all things are possible, they see my approach as "a pie in the sky platitude" that amounts to false hope. On the contrary. The conventional wisdom of saying "You can't have everything" is the real dream killer. Let me explain.

I've been asked what is it that I know for sure. Two things:

1. When you believe all things are possible, you give yourself a shot, however small, for that possibility.
2. You increase your odds of achieving success when you do a probability assessment.

I think I can play decent basketball. My big dream was always to play center for the Los Angeles Lakers. However, unless I grow another foot relatively quickly (I'm only 6 feet) and really tighten up on my dunking skills, I won't be playing alongside Kobe Bryant. Science says it's possible. Probability says, not likely. When I make these kinds of assessments, I put together a realistic map of what can be done in my life. If I start off by saying I can't have everything (or even worse, telling others they can't have everything), I deny myself and them the opportunity to explore what is possible. When I say to myself "I can't have everything", I don't even give myself a shot.

What fuels dreams and alternative options in our lives is the mere act of exploring other ways if one way seems closed. The "shut down" statement of "you can't have everything" takes away even the smallest fighting chance.

You may not catch me doing sky hooks in the yellow and purple, but chances are, you'll see me doing some pretty impressive things on the floor at the nearest 24-Hour fitness center. I'll take that alternative.

#27. Think this: I'll see it when I believe it. Not that: I'll believe it when I see it.

One of the challenges faced by my students is that they based almost everything on what they see. If they can't see it, it doesn't exist. In a materialist world, that conventional wisdom is pretty close to gospel.

The power of belief is that it allows you to see things that the current circumstances tend to obscure. In class we regularly do visioning exercises so that we get used to seeing things with our minds first and relying on physical vision second.

This kind of thinking may seem exceptional, but the truth is we do it all the time when we dream, when we daydream or when we imagine. All we did was give this process some discipline..

#28. Think this: That which a man soweth, he shall also reap. Not that: That which a man soweth, he shall also reap.

I didn't make a mistake. Let me explain.

When I was back in college, I was a good student, but I did some knucklehead stuff, too. Hey, it was college.

So to atone for my sins, I went to church. Sure enough, I'm in the second to the front row and the minister is laying down the law. In the middle of his fire and brimstone discourse, he looked directly at me and said, "That which a man soweth, he shall also reap!!" I was terrified. Could he have seen some of the knucklehead stuff I had done over the past week? Yikes!

I went home that morning with a heavy heart, full of guilt and shame. As I lay on my bed that night, his words kept repeating in my mind—that which a man soweth, he shall also reap. Then, it hit me—that phrase was not just a statement of condemnation. It was also a promise. That which a man soweth, he shall also reap! No matter what knucklehead stuff I did, there was a promise that I can reap the rewards of great things if I sow those seeds.

The following Sunday I saw the minister again. He looked at me with that same condemning scowl, and I just smiled right back at him. I understood his words from a whole new place.

I share this story with the students just so that they

can see how our interpretation of words can make all the difference as to how those words serve us or work against us. It all depends on our point of view. Those are seeds worth sowing.

#29. Think this: Bring the noise, bring the funk. Not that: Always color inside the lines.

I constantly challenged the students to step into levels of boldness about their lives. This boldness doesn't require them to be loud or demonstrative, but it does require them to give a damn about their lives and their place in the world. From understanding more about some of the students by talking with the support team at the shelter, I found that a lot of the challenges many of the students faced were self-inflicted wounds. There were things they could do something about, but they were too detached to do them. So in the stream of my classes I encourage the students to live their lives like they mean it, to embrace the current space and step into the world with boldness. Now some of this may seem like hyperbole, but the purpose is to make them become active participants in their human experience instead of observers. Sometimes that meant the difference between toning it down and bringing the noise. I'd ask "Did being on lock down work for you?" If it did, stay with it. If it didn't, may I suggest a new, more rigorous approach."

Many of the students liked this new way because it was an energetic, dynamic way of countering a long, slow numbing death march. Coloring outside the lines to bring the noise and the funk brought some students to reclaim their dreams and put meaning to their existence.

Sometimes, you gotta shake stuff up.

#30. Think this: Life has many different phases. Not that: Some people are busts.

I've had a chance to watch a sports program some years ago that talked about all time greatest sports busts. Busts are those folks that a lot of people have great expectations for, but the person doesn't live up to the hype. Thus, they are called busts.

Many of my students voiced the idea that they had the potential, but never lived up to it, so they considered themselves busts. In one class, a student told me that his family thought he was a bust. I told him I strongly disagreed with his family.

I told him that the beauty of being a so-called bust is that you have an opportunity to reflect, recalculate and re-boot your life going forward. The greatest opportunities that lie in front of you can only be seen when you leave the unrealistic, unrelenting, unforgiving world of the hype. Often, the bust is actually a boom. You can leave the pedestal, get your life back, and take the pressure off. That sounds like a pretty good deal to me.

Sometimes, the clearest path to the top can be seen looking up from the bottom.

#31. Think this: I am spiritual, but not religious. Not that: I am XYZ Religion.

Since the advent of online dating, the phrase "I'm spiritual but not religious" has become common.

The challenge many of my students face is that the constraints of their religion complicate their experience. While religion has the potential of being a port in the middle of a personal storm, most people use it as straitjacket in a very difficult asylum. The difficulties come when the student has an idea of how their religion would help him/her based on the formula dictated by religion. The obvious problem results when things didn't work out according to that formula. The religious person is left with four fixes:

1. Assigning the catch phrase "God works in mysterious ways"
2. Ignoring the contradiction altogether
3. Blaming the inconsistency on the devil
4. Becoming an atheist

None of these four "fixes" helps them solve the problem immediately. My experience tells me that this where many of the students suffered emotional breakdowns. Not having their challenges addressed according to formula is too hard to handle.

My fix is to create a more expanded version of their relationship with their faith by embracing their foundational religion, but also making room for their religion to act outside of what their formula would otherwise say. I call this extra-religious application spirituality.

I'm not the only person who is stepping outside of the thousands of religions in the world to help answer pressing challenges. According to a comprehensive national survey released last year by the Program on Public Values at Trinity College, "no religion" Americans are the only religious demographic that's growing in every single state. In a 2009 survey by the research firm LifeWay Christian Resources, 72 percent of millennials (18- to 29-year olds) said they're "more spiritual than religious." There are as many Americans identifying as "no religion" as there are mainline Christians, Jews, and Mormons in the United States combined.

It was my own personal pursuit of faith that led me to spend the last 9 years of my life volunteering at a homeless shelter in Denver, Colorado. It is my spirituality, however, which forces me to do the work to find out what I believe and not rely on edicts provided to me through an organized structure. That's not to say religion does not promote rigorous pursuit of faith, but to be spiritual means that you had to think about what you believe as opposed to have it handed to you through tradition.

Is there self-centeredness and complacency in being spiritual instead of religious? Yes, I know that's true. But I'm kinda thinking that's just part of the human condition, because you'll also find that in organized religion, too.

Shift Tool

2

Empower Yourself Like A Grocery Store

Supermarket stores are not just nice, benign ways of picking up tonight's dinner or your prescriptions. They are masterfully- crafted marketing tools that seek to persuade you to do something-- preferably, spend more of your hard-earned dollars with them. You may not like what they do, but their methods are effective. Let me share with you a few tricks of the trade you can use in the development of your personal space. You may find them effective in implementing for your organization as well.

A.   *From The Front To The Back*: Ever wonder why the staples of bread, milk and meat are in the very back of the store instead of in the front where you can easily get to them? After all, those staples are the most requested items by you and other shoppers. The supermarkets know this, so placing those items in the back forces you to go all the way through the store to get to them. Hopefully, as you walk through the store, you'll pick up another item or two that you didn't plan on getting when you first set out to go to the store. Trust me, this method works.

How can you use this method for your own empowerment? I'm glad you asked. Put your most active room in your house down the basement or way in the back of your home. Between the door you enter and that room, place personal empowerment sayings on the walls along the way. That way, those sayings will be something you see before you get to that room. We often place empowerment and inspirational sayings in rooms where they look nice. That's great if you're an interior decorator, but we want to maximize their effectiveness. Put them in places where you travel the most in your house.

Supermarkets often place sale signs and specials in those aisles. This keeps your mind from becoming used to seeing them and start tuning those items out. You can do the same by switching placement of your sayings in different places, but along the same well-travelled hallways. Do this once a month.

B. **Eye-Level Placement**: Ever notice when you walk in a supermarket that brand name items are at eye level and the generics are down toward the bottom? There's a method to that madness. If you make a brand of corn flakes and you want a supermarket to sell it, you pay them extra money so that they will place those items at eye level. That's why brand named items cost more. You're paying for their marketing placement. You are much more likely to purchase items you see at eye level (which is about 5 ft 6 in.—the average height of a woman) than those items you actually have to do some work to see. Make sure you place those empowerment signs at eye level. If they are not at eye level, the chances of you seeing them and remembering them reduce dramatically.

C. **Waiting Areas**: Ever wonder why there are so few checkers at the supermarket when there are so many people trying to check out? Besides the supermarket folks trying to save money, they know that the longer you wait in line, the higher the chance is that you'll think of something else to get, or even more, you'll buy one of those items they place in the check-out line. Yep, that's what happens. If there is a place where you do a lot of waiting or leisurely activity in your home, put more affirmation statements. Your eyes will wander if you're at the computer for a period of time and start to look around the room. Give your eyes something to read while you're waiting. A quick glace of your affirmation statement can be very effective in affecting your subconscious.

Use your space to tell yourself what you already agree is true for you. What's happening here is basic programming, but not at the hands of someone else. You are doing the programming.

Quantum Physics and Science

#32. Think this: Quantum Physics is what's up. Not that: Newtonian Science is the foundation of all we know.

If the field of science was a high school, Newtonian Science would be the popular smart kid who also happens to be the homecoming king. Quantum Physics would be the new, weird kid that was not quite comfortable in her own skin, but was smarter than the Newtonian Science kid and cool enough to attract the attention of her classmates because of her tattoos, funky hair and piercings. Quantum Physics is another path set by science in an attempt to explain what's happening in the world around us. The difference between the two schools of thought is that one (Newtonian Science) does not, cannot or will not account for stuff we can't explain or even understand right now. Quantum Physics has the audacity to try to explain the stuff using the most far out ideas and theorems, and is cool if you don't like it.

Where Newtonian Science sees itself at odds with spirituality, Quantum Physics makes spirituality look reasonable and comfortable without losing its stride as a discipline. Where Newtonian science needs tangible evidence for its structure to work, Quantum Physics can stretch that need beyond what we would call "reality".

The application of Quantum Physics with people wrestling with homelessness and joblessness is simple: there's a bigger world of possibilities out there that's stranger, mightier, and stronger than you think.

There is also a kind of "cool" factor when you're breaking down Superstring theory to some people who barely got their GED. I remember one of my students telling me how he shared this with his family: "I told them I was learning Quantum Physics and they said, 'Really? Can we come too?'"

Quantum theory is cool like that.

I don't claim to be a professor type who can technically break down this stuff in the language of the trade. I leave that to my brother who is a PhD in biotechnology. On the contrary, my best asset is being a lay person, seeking to make all of this science stuff tangible and applicable in the world the rest of us live in.

If you've spent any time watching the Discovery Channel, the History Channel, or read *The Elegant Universe* or even catching some of the Sci-Fi movies, you know Quantum Mechanics/Physics is now a part of our pop culture jargon. Parallel universes, quantum leaps, the Butterfly Effect, String Theory, wormholes and warp drive all come from this emerging science. Its growing popularity is directly linked to our questions about the universe and our place in it. Simply put, we've outgrown Newtonian science. However, any self-respecting physicist will tell you that Quantum Physics doesn't invalidate Newtonian Science. On the contrary, it only means we've established the link between the two, and are now ready to take the relationship to the next level. It would be like the homecoming king and the new weird kid are going out on a date, but she's driving.

#33. Think this: Drake's Equation—We are not alone. Not that: We are the only creatures in the universe.

In my last book, I mentioned this exercise is one I've come to really enjoy with students. The students play the role of President of the United States.   Aliens land in the back lawn of the White House and appear only to the president and his/her Cabinet. They say "Hey, we're here and just wanted to say, 'What's up?'" Then, they take off. The question is, do you go on television and tell the world what you experienced, or do you keep it to yourself? By a 2-to-1 margin, the students say don't tell them.

When I ask why, the students respond something like "because the people wouldn't be ready for that kind of information. They would just freak out and break down".

At this point, I remind the students of how important it is to research, talk about and visualize their new life going forward because if they don't, they'll suffer the same fate. If we don't prepare ourselves to take in new information by expanding our capacity, we will tax our belief system and it will break down under the stress.

Back in 1960, Physicist Frank Drake wanted to expand

the capacity of his scientific colleagues by bringing something to the table to a professional meeting. Drake knew that if we are ever to be prepared to meet people from another planet, we have to at least contemplate the idea in the scientific community with a theory that says it's possible we're not alone. As a matter of fact, Drake said there were at least 10,000 different civilizations in our Galaxy alone, and wrote a scientific formula to support his position. His formula goes a little something like this:

$$N = R^* \times f_p \times n_e \times f_\ell \times f_i \times f_c \times L$$

Eh…yeah.

Remember, Frank Drake is a trained professional. Kids, don't try this at home.

Teaching the principle of Drake's equation helped the students understand that building capacity is a necessary process when trying to wrap your head around an idea that's "alien" to your sense of reality—even one as exotic as visitors from another planet or as provincial as moving from a life of limited options to one of endless possibilities.

#34. Think this: Ockham's Razor—The simplest solution is usually the correct one. Not that: It's complicated.

Ockham's razor sometimes spelled Occam's razor is a principle attributed to the 14th-century English logician and Franciscan friar, William of Ockham. The principle states that in the explanation of any phenomenon, we should make as few assumptions as possible. Translation: All other things being equal, the simplest answer is usually the correct one.

One weekend night when I was 16, my parents decided to go down to Des Moines, Iowa, with friends. They left the car at the house with me and my four siblings with specific instructions that their car was not to be touched.

Ah, the foolishness of youth....

Of course, as they left, I found my father's extra set of keys and decided to take a risky journey to go see my girlfriend. Funny, as I look back now, it was like watching an episode of the *Flintstones*. You just knew Fred's plan was not going to work, but it was like watching a slow moving train wreck— you couldn't turn away. The car was low on gas and I drove to the gas station. A knucklehead turn at the gas pump lead to a serious scratch on the back end of the car. For the first time in my 16 years of living, I felt the cold grip of death around my throat as I contemplated my father's discovery of my misdeed. "I didn't even have sex yet" was my first thought as I took inventory of all the things I did accomplish in this short, yet now terminal existence. I drove the car back, tried to put some shine on the scratch and then prayed like a Pentecostal preacher at a tent revival. "God, if you'll make it like it didn't happen, I'll quit sneaking from morning church service to hang out with those Union Baptist girls at Reed's store." (A pretty serious prayer because the Union Baptist girls were gorgeous!).

I think I fell asleep on my knees.

My folks came back that night.

A day passed. Nothing was said. Another day passed. Nothing.

On the third day, my father asked me at breakfast about a scratch on his car. He did it in a calm, yet determined way. I found myself throwing every theory against the wall to see if something would stick. The idea was that if I could just throw an element of doubt in the mix, just to muddy the waters (like a defense attorney), I could keep Pops confused. Let me see if I can remember some of the things I said:

- I told him of a story of my younger brother Wade moving a bicycle in the garage and how we got into a fight, which resulted in the scratch on the car.

- I told him it could have been from some situation that happened before he left town and he didn't notice it at the time when it happened.

- I told him it might have happened when I was going to wash his car but scratched the car as I was taking out the wash equipment.

Each one of these stories was elaborate with a lot of details and variables in them. My father just looked at me as I squirmed like a worm on a hook. He knew that the more elaborately I lied, the more I was guilty. I knew my task was fruitless. I felt like I was going to the chair and my dad was asking me if I had any last words. At the end of my testimony, I just broke down and told him what really happened. I said "It was me, Dad, I did it! I'm sorry."

I could never be a spy. They wouldn't have to waterboard me. A few minutes of silence from my interrogator and I'd be singing like Luther Vandross, especially if that interrogator was my dad. The silence was my dad's own form of "enhanced rendition."

He didn't punish me, but he did use the "d" word. You know, disappointed. He then gave me the silent treatment for a few days.

Every time I think of Ockham's Razor I think of that scenario and how many times we create elaborate explanations about things going on in our lives, when the simplest explanation is the correct one. It's us.

When many my students first come to the class, they spend a lot of time explaining how they ended up in the shelter. Of course, it wasn't their fault. It was kind of like going to prison and listening to prisoners tell their story— they were innocent victims of circumstances. The people who told the longest stories always had at least 3 other people involved. The shortest stories were the people who said, "I'm responsible for my situation. I made poor choices." Simple. To the point. Uncomplicated.

Saying that it's us is not a condemnation of us or what we did; it's a way of taking responsibility for our part. Simplifying everything to the equation that it starts and ends with us only means we take ownership for ALL of our life—not some of it, or the parts we find convenient or the parts we don't like. It means all of it. I like to say that if it happened on our watch, it's ours.

#35. Think this: It's all about Schrodinger's cat. Not that: It's all about Pavlov's dog.

For the record, I'm a dog guy. I've always loved dogs. I like cats, but they just don't respond like dogs. In this case, however, I have become a cat guy because of what Schrodinger's cat represents.

I rolled this out to my students one class because one of the newcomers to the class said that he felt his life was already pre-determined to be difficult and there was nothing he could do about it. The Schrodinger's Cat thought experiment explanation seemed like an appropriate application to his blues about his fate.

Every armchair psychologist will use some reference to the Pavlov's dog experiment because of the work of Russian psychologist Ivan Pavlov. This eminent scientist developed the idea of classical conditioning, where certain things would trigger certain responses in people and animals. He first tried the experiment on his dog. We've been referencing that experiment in casual conversation ever since.

Now enter Erwin Schrodinger. His thought experiment involving his cat is becoming all the rage because how it relates to how we are connected to all things and all outcomes. In a nutshell, Schrodinger proposed a scenario with his cat in a sealed box, wherein the cat and a flask of cyanide were put in a box. Before Schrodinger opens the box to see the cat's fate, the cat is both dead and alive at the same time. When Schrodinger opens the box to check on his cat, only one version of the cat's fate is observed. But before he opened the box, all possibilities of the cat's fate existed at the same time. To bring this down into every day terms, the things that happen in our world are not separate from us. We are "entangled" with all possible outcomes. Once we see ourselves as being part of the outcome of what we observe, we will see ourselves as active "entangled" participants of our world, instead of non-participants, watching from the sidelines.

I can't tell you how sharing this basic Quantum Physics paradox theory helps my students wrap their heads around the idea that "many worlds" are possible, even in the world they live in, despite how it appears to them.

And in a shout out to my friends at PETA—to the best of my knowledge, no cat or dog was harmed during these experiments or in the writing of this book.

#36. Think this: I'm subscribing to exopolitics. Not that: It's all about geopolitics.

I've always been intrigued by science and space, even though I sucked at calculus. I guess I'm more intrigued by the social application of scientific ideas than I am with the math. There is one scientific field on the rise that I share with the students because of how it may directly affect their quality of life in the near future.

Over the past couple of years, a very quiet evolution has been happening in the world. Brazil, Sweden, Mexico, Russia, France, Canada, the UK, and other countries have been marching toward a policy of disclosure on what they know about—brace yourself—Unidentified Flying Objects. The reports these countries are now releasing were previously classified as top secret, but are now being provided to the general public. Sure, a lot of the really juicy stuff is probably redacted, but it still points to the fact that a quantifiable, verifiable phenomena is happening around the world and we finally get access to some of that information. These reports contain a lot of credible and highly trained eyewitness reports, coming from police officers, military personnel and commercial pilots as well as civilians. While many of those reports were explained away as previously unknown weather phenomena, experimental military aircraft, or optical illusions, a significant number of all of those items were classified as "unknown" because they could not be explained from the current science we have at our disposal today.

Why are governments around the world (save the U.S.) now sharing what they know at this point in time? The answer may be people power. A number of credible private and public citizens are charging forward to get ahead of this discussion.

Exopolitics is the emerging discipline that formalizes the

discussion of public policy toward visitors from other planets and how their presence could impact life as we know it. What will extraterrestrial life visiting our planet mean to our energy policy? What about nation-state borders? Security? What about religion?

For those of you who simply couldn't fathom the idea that we could be visited by beings from another planet, let me entertain a more provincial view. It is possible that we are not being visited and that the hundreds of thousands of witnesses who are seeing these craft and beings are actually seeing new, experimental projects by someone's military. This still begs similar questions:

- Whose government is behind this?

- What is the purpose of this technology? Is it benign or malicious?

- If they have this technology and this new energy source, why aren't they sharing it with the rest of us to end our dependency on fossil fuel?

- What about our nation-state borders? If they can zip around anywhere at anytime and be witnessed by hundreds of trained observers, does this pose a national security challenge?

Just because they may not be visitors from another planet doesn't mean that we're not facing the most profound questions in the history of humankind.

Chances are good you'll be hearing this word kicked around for the foreseeable future as disclosure efforts start to speed up over the next few years.

And if you feel a need to put foil over your head to keep the aliens from reading your thoughts, knock yourself out.

#37. Think this: I believe in survival of those who are able to adapt. Not that: I believe in survival of the fittest.

I joke with my students that if the world should ever deteriorate into an apocalyptic war and the planet devastated, they would be the remaining survivors. Why? Because they have learned to do what so many cannot—they have learned to adapt to their surroundings and situation for survival. They may have had a job, wife and kids, then everything changed. But that change gives them strength lacking in so many others. When people think about the old saying "survival of the fittest," so famously attributed to Darwin's theory of evolution, they are missing the core of what he was trying to communicate in that theory. If you read Darwin's work, particularly *The Origin Of Species*, the central theme is that the fittest is not the strongest or the smartest. The fittest are the ones who are most able to adapt and survive in changing environments. Our world is so enamored with strength and size, we miss the fact that cockroaches are not even .001 our size, yet have been around longer than we have, and probably will outlive us in the end. Their ability to adapt makes them the fittest.

Chances are, our infatuation with big and strong and translating that as being the best able to survive may have something to do with the Industrial Revolution. Bigger, stronger, more powerful was the way of the world in the late

1800s through the early 1900s. However, that was only for a very brief period of time compared to the long view of life. Just ask the big, bad, strong dinosaurs.

Ooops. I forgot, we can't ask them—they're not around anymore.

Put a billionaire and a 10-year homeless person in the middle of a world that's been destroyed and no infrastructure exists. Who would you put your money on to survive?

In some ways, the Sustainability Movement and those who think it's just bunk is really a discussion between the fittest of our societies and those not so fit. The fittest are asking the question, "How do we adapt and survive in a world that really has changed from what we knew just a few years ago?" The not-so-fit are saying, "I want to keep things the same or return things to the way they were a few years ago." Listen to what your friends are saying around this and you'll be able to figure out who will be around in a few years.

#38. Think this: *Star Trek*'s James T. Kirk was a diplomatic captain. Not that: *Star Trek*'s Jean-Luc Picard was the diplomat. Kirk was the cowboy.

Okay, indulge me for a hot minute.

My students knew I was a Trekkie and would sometimes jokingly savage Captain James T. Kirk just to mess with me.

I think Kirk gets a bad rap when it comes to his style as captain of the *Enterprise*. Trekkers say he fought first and talked later, while Jean-Luc Picard started off with protocol pleasantries and diplomatic conversation. But when I look back at all of the episodes, Kirk was involved in just as many negotiations as Picard. Their styles were just a bit different. Kirk was involved in what we would now call "aggressive negotiations," yet they were negotiations nevertheless.

Don't hate on Kirk!

#39. Think this: The Heisenberg Principle of Uncertainty can help us direct our lives. Not that: Things are unchangeable and immovable.

I love bringing quantum physics into the classroom with people in transition. I find it extremely helpful to stretch my student's minds above and beyond all that they knew, then bring it back to them in a tangible, practical way. The Heisenberg Principle of Uncertainty is one of those quantum physics tools that is well received.

The Heisenberg uncertainty principle states that the more we know about where a particle is, the less we know about the speed and direction the particle is traveling, or vice versa. In other words, since all things are made of particles, we really don't know what we're seeing because it can't be measured. Everything is in a constantly moving, dynamic state. We are "uncertain" where those things are.

Going further, what I propose to my students is a basic question—if we don't know what we're seeing because it can't be measured, what can we say is truly real? Since the trouble we're seeing in our lives is in flux, why not change it to something better? Since everything is dynamic and in a state of flux, can't we also direct our lives to something great?

Once I would see that blank stare on their faces, I'd bring it back to the everyday: "Based on the current science, your lives are flexible, changeable and in flux. You can direct your lives any way you want it to go. It is up to you. The one thing that is real is your state of belief about your life."

This helps students understand the importance of what they were thinking and how all things can be changed or rearranged if we believe.

I simply can't think of a more rewarding experience than going through these discussions with people going through homelessness. It is rich to see the "aha" light bulb come on, and I am fortunate to be there to witness it.

3 *Shift Tool*

Beware Of The Quick Fix

I often tell the story of what happened when me and my then wife were expecting our first child, Chet Mario. As I was driving her to the hospital, she was in a great deal of pain (as these things usually go). We finally got there. As she was going into surgery, Michelle said with great passion: "You did this to me. This is crazy, I won't do this again." She tried to get me to promise her that we won't have another child. Obviously I told her I couldn't make that promise. As all 9.3 pounds of Mario finally came out through Caesarean section, I cut the cord, bathed him and wrapped him in swaddling clothes. As I took him up to his mom, a big beautiful smile broke across her face. She talked about how beautiful he was and said, "Can we have another one?"

That's what happens when we're experiencing shift. The pain of the shift can be very intense, primarily because we don't want to let go of that which we've known. The first temptation is always to go back to the tried and tested, or to make ourselves promises to maintain the status quo. Be aware of the deals you make with yourself and with others during shift periods. They may not be the deal you want and they may be deals made under duress or high stress. The key is to be aware that it can happen.

By the way, two years later we had another son, Chase Maliq Langston Sisk, all 8.9 pounds of him.

Money

#40. Think this: I'm a contract worker. Not that: I have a full-time job with benefits.

One of the things employers discovered on the other side of the recent world recession is that they could become more efficient by employing contract or temporary workers instead of full time employees. This development has been happening for a long time, but really gained steam after this last economic downturn.

In 2005, the U.S. government estimated that 31% of American workers were already so-called contingent workers. Experts say that number could increase to 40% or more in the next 10 years.

James Stoeckmann, senior practice leader at WorldatWork, a professional association of human resource executives, believes that full-time employees could become the minority of the nation's workforce within 20 to 30 years, leaving employees without traditional benefits such as health coverage, paid vacations and retirement plans, that most workers take for granted today.

"The traditional job is not doomed. But it will increasingly have competition from other models, the most prominent is the independent contractor model," he said.

Some of you are saying, "That doesn't apply to me, Chet. I have a good job with benefits that I've been at for a while." Cool. But let me ask you this: when was the last time you were at a job longer than 2 to 3 years? Even those of us with full-time jobs are really contract workers. Your particular contract is just a little longer and with more benefits than those who are doing a 6-weeks to 6-months gig. With this in mind, the employment choices you make should be based around the question: "How can this job help me get my next job?"

I share this knowledge with my students after I realized many of them were still planning their reestablishment around the idea of nailing down a traditional full-time job with benefits. Once they understand that the terrain has changed significantly, even over the past few years, it helps them prepare more effectively. When they started seeing themselves as independent contractors, it opened a ton of new doors to them. They actually saw themselves differently.

It can be argued this new approach is creating more uncertainty in our world, but it seems that our best source of security will come when we make ourselves valuable in the work arena and create a demand for our services.

#41. Think this: True wealth is in Balance Sheet Affluence. Not that: Get rich quick.

Like clockwork, a student at some point in my class would infer that rich people are evil.

I've worked with both the rich and the poor. I can assure you, there are plenty of knuckleheads in both camps. Rich people are evil is just a part of old groupthink, perpetuated by conventional wisdom. The new conventional wisdom has moved from getting rich to being human wealthy. This particular shift should satisfy both sides of this socioeconomic chasm. The difference between getting rich and becoming human wealthy is that getting rich focuses on obtaining money. Becoming human wealthy considers the more important indexes of true wealth, such as quality of life, relationships, social involvement in community, volunteerism and good health. A person who scores well in those categories can live a more fulfilling life, no matter what their economic conditions dictate.

Some people have called this movement "Balance Sheet Affluence." Here are some of the questions to contemplate your Balance Sheet Affluence status:

- If all of your debts were called in today, would you have the money to pay them off?
- If you looked at your diet right now, would you be able to say you eat more healthy food than unhealthy food?

- If you were to pass away today, would you have more detractors or admirers at your funeral?
- If you were asked today, would you be able to say you have more happy days than sad ones?
- Do you have more friends or more enemies?
- Do you have more drugs or more preventative care supplements in your house?
- If you were at the end of your life right now, would you be able to say you've done more good than harm?

You get the idea. These are the new measuring sticks I offer my students so that they would quit chasing money and start being wealthy. These tools to wealth are much more accessible than tons of money.

When you start taking account of those numbers, you'll find out if you are human wealthy or are living in human poverty. This is the balance sheet.   Despite the allure of making tons of money, another definition is starting to emerge that is focused on quality of our humanity.

When you make your next 2-, 3- or 5-year plan, be sure to include tools that will increase your human wealth as well as your money.

#42. Think this: Money can't buy happiness. Not that: People are most motivated by money.

If you give money to homeless people and panhandlers who ask you for it on street corners, you're not helping. You are perpetuating the problem. I know you feel that you're doing the right thing, but you're not helping. If giving money would solve the problem of homelessness, you would have fewer people asking for a handout, not more.

Other homeless people tell me this.

Our society has been fixated on the idea that we can solve most of our problems by throwing money at it. Our reasoning is that once people have enough money, they'll leave the field of panhandling and begging. As we have all discovered, that isn't the case. Money by itself simply isn't enough to motivate people beyond what they're doing.

It appears that the human spirit has another set of criteria that motivates us to change and a greater life. According to Arnold Kling, the author of *The Materialism Fallacy*, economists finally woke up to the reality that people make decisions based not only on available resources but also according to their beliefs. Notions such as the importance of trust, relativity of risk, and perceptions of the immediate family, peers, culture on trade, are recent arrivals to scientific inquiries and economic policies.

In my sessions at the shelter, I do a class called "The Vision Party." In the class, a student gets up in front of the class and talks about their greatest desire in this life. Some of the visions included going back to school, opening a coffee house, fly fishing, writing a book and operating a daycare center. 97% of the time, no one visualizes having a lot of money. And these are the very people who most would say need money the most. It's not that money isn't important. It's just that money is not the ultimate goal. With this in mind, I help the students concentrate on the ultimate vision so that they wouldn't get confused by money along the way. As a friend of mine most deftly put it—the main thing, is to keep the main thing the main thing.

I'm certainly not saying that money can't buy things. It can. And lot of things at that. But as humankind continues to mature, we're discovering that there is a cap on the level of contentment it can produce. It simply can't buy happiness.

#43. Think this: You are your biggest and best investment. Not that: Buying a home is your biggest and best investment.

People who are homeless often feel that they are second-class citizens because they don't own a home. Even when they become renters, there is a kind of smugness in our society that separates renters from "owners" and homeless people feel that quiet narrative directly. So in order to give the students some perspective about home ownership, I re-direct their attention to the most important investment that's more important than a house: themselves.

I first reveal some things a lot of people may not fully appreciate about home ownership. Let's do the math.

Let's say you decide to buy a $500,000 home with $100,000 saved for the down payment or deposit....

Check the key numbers:
Home price = $500,000

Deposit / down payment = $100,000
Loan = $400,000
Interest rate = 5%
Loan period = 30 years

Got a loan calculator? Plug these numbers and you'll discover the following:

Monthly repayments (interest and principal) = $1,666.66
Total interest payable over 30 years = $600,000
Total amount payable over 30 years = $1,000,000

So, where's the "investment" when you're paying an extra $600,000 on top of the price of the home?

Everyone and their grandmother bought into this conventional wisdom, often without running the numbers. Things are changing. In 2003, 83 percent of those interviewed in a similar study by Fannie Mae said real estate was a safe investment, compared with about 70 percent in the most recent survey in 2010. Of course some of this is because of the recent recession, but there are indications this is a far deeper shift is occurring. At the same time, the hottest growth area throughout the world is personal development seminars and workshops. Adult education is right behind it. It's as if we figured out that the rainbow that shows the way to the pot of gold leads right back to us.

Sure, banks and other commercial organizations treat you differently when you're a home owner (more accurately a "home buyer," as the home is actually owned by the bank as collateral until you pay off the loan), and you could count the intangibles that go along with it as valuable. But the conventional wisdom that it is your best investment is finally giving way to something that makes more sense. You.

Education, entrepreneurship, personal development, training and hard work add immensely to your value and long-term earning power in the work field. All of this is without an interest rate. Even more, your development is not on loan from a bank. You own it, and no one can take it from you. You can even use this investment well into your retirement years if you'd like. It has no limiting shelf life.

The message I relay in class is that renting, and spending your time in your personal development, may allow you to take the savings you would otherwise put into your home into something more fun, like a trip around the world or annual family reunions or going back to school. Don't get me wrong. I am an advocate for ownership, but only if it makes sense.

Your home is not only not your best investment, it's not an investment at all. It's a place to live, a place to make your own, and a place to make yours. It's a place to put down roots, a place to raise a family, and a place to grow old in. It's a place to call your own, it's just not an investment. It's a home.

#44. Think this: Corporate welfare is gouging the system. Not that: Minority welfare mothers are gouging the system.

People going through homelessness would sometimes

see themselves as the enemy. They would often talk about themselves in disparaging ways, probably because society does. Modern conventional wisdom has something to do with that. Many people think that homeless people are homeless because they are lazy welfare robbers who don't want to work. From almost 10 years of working on the ground level I can say that narrative is simply not true. Yes, there are those who have chosen a lifestyle that doesn't involve work, but I have met people like that who are rich as well.

I have a sneaking suspicion that if we could get away with it, none of us would work, either.

In order to get the students to see themselves differently, I give them a more honest explanation of how welfare operates in the US.

The CIA has a system called "The Mighty Wurlitzer". It is one of their methods of affecting public opinion by repeating an idea over and over again in numerous places until the public believes what it's hearing must be true. This conventional wisdom about poor people being welfare robbers has been repeated so regularly, it is intimately imbedded in the U.S. subconscious. Any information countering this concept would seem bizarre.

Allow me to share some bizarre data.

According to the U.S. Office for Management and Budget in 2008, the amount of money provided to individuals in the U.S. for food stamps, family support assistance, temporary assistance to needy families and child nutrition programs, while not including Medicaid and Social Security, is around $117 billion. Let's compare this with the amount of welfare corporations get from the U.S. government.

- According to the OMB, in 2008 the total amount for corporate entitlement (welfare) programs were $354.3 billion.

- The Cato Institute, a Libertarian think tank, estimates that federal aid to corporations ranges from $250 billion to $350 billion a year. It has specifically identified 125 federal programs subsidizing private businesses that would save taxpayers $85 billion if cut.

- According to recent Congressional Budget Office statistics, total federal spending on a safety net for the poor costs the average taxpayer about $400 a year, while spending on corporate welfare programs costs the same taxpayer about $1,400 a year.

- According to the organization Citizens for Tax Justice: Most social spending is in the form of discretionary spending, which is scrutinized in the annual budget negotiating process in Congress; most corporate welfare programs are in the form of tax expenditures, which go on and on since they are not subject to annual review by Congress.

It's not hard to find this information. What is hard to understand is how this information has been obscured from public dialogue, thus having a direct impact on the shaping of public policy toward the most defenseless people in the society.

Some of this may sound like I'm politicizing a deeply held traditional belief regarding welfare, but as my Journalism professor used to say, "If you want to find the truth, just follow the money."

#45. Think this: People look for more value during down times. Not that: People tend to spend on vices and lower-priced things during down times.

Tell the truth, many of you have been going to Walmart a few more times than usual due to the tough economic times.

Don't front. I know you have. I probably saw a few of you there myself.

The conventional wisdom is that when people are stressed due to tough economic times, they leave Macy's and head over to Walmart for the cheap stuff. That's partly true. We are looking around at bargain stores, but only if we can find better value for an item. In a May 2010 report from *Fortune Magazine*, the "Great Recession" redefined spending patterns, creating a new way to think about how we shop. Instead of merely trading down and spending impulsively, people shopped smarter, honing in on the products they actually desired and reallocating their budgets to make such purchases possible. This trend actually has been happening for some time. It seems that the 'Great Recession' expedited the process.

My students introduced me to an even more effective

ways of getting more value for their money. Here are some of their tips:

- Go to the Dollar stores, but only the ones that actually say "everything is only a dollar."

- Goodwill has better service and quality items than The Salvation Army.

- Double down on your coupon power by using the coupons on items that are on sale that day.

- Buy a high-end car (e.g., BMW, Mercedes, Cadillac) at a used car dealership for a good price if it has 80,000 miles or less. This way you get value and at least two more good years from the vehicle.

All of this is part of the move to chic austerity, where we don't mind going less pricey as long as we know there's value in our purchase. Otherwise, the cheap stuff goes the same way of the expensive stuff—outta here.

#46. Think this: It takes creativity to make money. Not that: It takes money to make money.

People going through homelessness often lean on this crutch because of the universal nature of this conventional idea. You can't make money if you don't have money, so since I don't have money, I'll remain broke. In order to get them to access or tune in to the resources that were all around them, I had to at least get them to see that there was something wrong with the "takes money to make money" concept.

I don't know about you, but I can think of at least 5 friends who had all the resources (money) in the world, but couldn't leverage it into an ongoing profitable entity. At the same time, I also knew people who took at basic idea on an almost non-existent budget and made magic happen. Even my own advertising agency was a thought that came to me in a dream. I scraped together all of 1,500 dollars, printed some business cards, made a one-sheet explanation of my topical radio advertising process and headed to a newspaper conference where I locked my first four clients. All of this on the heels of the recession of the early 1990s.

Truth is, hard times have historically been the best times to make money. More than half of the 30 Dow Jones companies trace their birth to recessions. Hewlett-Packard, for example, which had revenues of $92 billion last year, was founded with just $6,000 (in 2007 dollars) in the wake of the Great Depression. And Bill Gates, who now has a net worth of $56 billion, was an unemployed college dropout when he founded Microsoft in the mid-'70s.

How can good economic things happen during so-called bad times? Hard times and/or having little money can bring out the most creative in us.

A perfect example is Ted Rheingold, CEO of Dogster. com. Rheingold launched his site in 2004 with $0, was turning a profit a year later, and now the site brings in more than $1 million annually. Compare that with Pets.com, which launched in 2000 with a monster $82.5 million initial public offering and was out of business within 9 months. The difference? Dogster was more nimble. Both companies were banking on pet accessories. But when no one wanted to buy them, Dogster quickly focused on providing social networking for pet lovers. Meanwhile, Pets.com was stuck with warehouses full of unsold chew toys.

The conspiracy theorist in me says some rich guy put out this conventional wisdom saying so that he could limit his competition. The more people who believed that, the less opposition he faced to his own enterprise. If you were believing it, he already took you out of the game. But if you didn't buy it, he now had to look over his shoulder. The more the students realized they had creativity and innovation on their side, the more they started figuring out that the resources to make that idea a reality would come. Our odds of overcoming odds increase dramatically once we recognize the true tool that we all have, whether we're rich or poor—it's creativity.

#47. Think this: "Good Debt" is not necessarily good. Not that: Debt helps us live a quality life.

We often talk about money in this class, primarily from a philosophical perspective. I give plenty of details about the life I led during the reign of my advertising agency. I told them how, when my company was flush, banks were throwing money at me. I always thought how odd it was that I could get money when I didn't need it, but when I needed it most, I couldn't get it. I understand the process, but what I found disturbing most of all was how everyone from the banks to the credit card companies and others, sought ways of helping me extend my personal debt, quickly and easily. I was told that this was "good debt." One of my students responded, "That doesn't sound like a bad thing if you manage it right." Initially I agreed with him. But the more I looked into how debt is sold around the world, I had to give my students a more sober second perspective.

For the past two decades, a steady drumbeat of information has come from lending institutions explaining "good debt" vs. "bad debt" to a consumer society in the States and other parts of the world. The good debt is explained as ways to enhance life by borrowing money for important things like mortgages, college education and starting businesses. The "bad debt" is money used to purchase things that go down in value.

On the surface, this seems fine, especially if you're focused on paying off the debt quickly. However, the gentle push by the lending organization is not to have you pay off the debt quickly, but to extend your ongoing perpetual indebtedness. The lending institution simply doesn't make the same money with a quick payoff as opposed to having you in a long, silent debt cycle. This silent debt cycle seems relatively painless to us, so we borrow over and over and over until many of us end up in a kind of debt slavery servitude. Most of our waking hours are geared around servicing the personal debt we've accumulated. Some people even mark their value in society with pride based on how much debt they have.

I don't want to be misquoted about this subject. I believe the challenge we have is not with the tool of borrowing and lending, but with the culture of borrowing and lending.

In ever-increasing numbers, financial advisors are changing their tune on debt. Business writer John Casparie with *Entrepreneur Magazine* wrote an article called, "Why Is Debt A Bad Thing?" and says monies owed over extended time can choke off the life of any business. For those of you (like me) who use Mint.com to manage your stuff, you'll be interested to know that the people at Mint wrote a report that asks the question "Does Good Debt Exist?".

Taleb Nassim, author of the book *The Black Swan* says people should have three sources of variation in their income so that they can reduce their cultural dependency on debt. The first one is to have their own business that they understand rather well. The second one is to have a robust savings plan. The third portion is the speculative portion: Whatever you are willing to lose, you can invest in whatever you want.

Sounds like a plan to me.

I started teaching this approach to my students simply because it is simple, accessible and not beyond their skill set. If they didn't start a business, we suggested that they position themselves as contractors who did their work on the side of their regular job. In the Black community, this is called a "hustle." "Everyone should have a hustle, just in case things get tough" is what my father used to say. I also strongly emphasized the students open a simple bank account and take advantage of the automatic savings plans banks are now pushing. Then, I told the students to keep some "play money" on the side. A few bucks over here in case friends or family asks you for help. You could loan it to them with interest, but not be devastated if the person doesn't pay you back. In a sense, you're investing in people. It may be highly speculative (depending on the people you're dealing with) but it is a form of investment.

My belief is that this approach will keep more and more people from falling into the debt trap that have brought so many of our clients to the shelter in the first place.

#48. Think this: The salary gap between men and women in the U.S. has disappeared. Not that: There is a salary gap between men and women in the U.S.

For the first few years of the class, I would often hear women who quit their jobs complain that they simply weren't being paid on the same scale as their male counterpoints. They would tell me it cost more to go to work than it would be to be unemployed at home and that gender bias was at the root of it all.

I would agree on this because everything I had read to that point clearly pointed to sexism in our working world. But recently I ran into information that has changed my tune and what I teach about sexism in the workplace going forward.

In a recent edition of *The Economist*, a full report on earnings across the board showed that a gender salary gap in America is gone. And many major U.S. news outlets have reported that women in their 20s are out-earning their male counterparts in large cities, which is not surprising because women are doing better in school than men are.

There is a gap that does still exists. Strangely enough, it's among holders of MBAs. The reason top-tier female MBAs make less than the men is because of the choice they make, not because of any gender bias. Women sometimes choose to stay at home with their children. They tend to work fewer hours per week, and they move in an out of the workforce more frequently than men do.

Even among those not so lucky to have a Harvard MBA, the salary gap is by choice: *The Christian Science Monitor* reported that 86% of women who left the workforce or downshifted did so because the workplace does not accommodate parenting. Men, of course, have the same problem—they are parents also—but they do not make that choice. That the workforce is not good for parenting just is not a gender issue.

There is the issue of class here when comparing my students to Harvard grads, but it is clear that pay between men and women as an issue is disappearing. She may be right about how it can be less expensive to stay home and collect unemployment than it is to work a job when you take in transportation and day care into consideration. That, however, sounds more like an issue relating to depressed wages all the way around, and less about gender-based discrimination. So instead of spending our class time on how to get companies to focus on paying women more, we focus on how to get the company to pay my student more, as well as how she could reduce her overall expenses.

I'll let you know how that's working out in the next book.

Shift Tool 4: Create Your Own Theorems And Philosophies

All conventional wisdom started off with some guy or gal making a statement somewhere. That's pretty powerful stuff when you think about how these random ideas and thoughts can morph into something powerful that has an influence on societal thinking and policy. With this in mind, allow me to suggest making up your own ideas, philosophies and theorems.

Why not?

You don't have to offer up your ideas for peer review or even see it as a great philosophical aid to society, but you can create your own set of ideas that can help you navigate your world more effectively. Check out a few of my own:

1. **The Goofiness Theory**—No matter how many times you provide clear instructions, someone will not follow them and ask you to explain it again.

2. **The Love Principle**—Love is always the answer.

3. **The Principle of The Ridiculous**—It's ridiculous to think that all things remain the same.

4. **The Bonus Fries Theory**—Just when you're thinking "Boy, those fries were good. I wish I had more," a few more fries can be found, miraculously, inside that bag.

5. **The "Thou Doth Protest Too Much" Razor**—Whoever is protesting the loudest about something is most likely guilty of it themselves.

6. **The Philosophy of Absolute Knuckleheadedness**—Only knuckleheads proclaim their ideas are absolute and beyond reproach.

7. **The Kitchen Rule**—No matter how inviting and stylish your living room and great room look, everyone still ends up in the kitchen.

8. **The *Star Trek* Landing-Party Extra Theory**—The extra guy on *Star Trek* away missions is always going to be victimized by the alien. If you don't become one of the main characters at the place where you work, chances are good you're gonna get written out of the scene, too.

This process helps us to understand trust and respect our own thinking more. Write a few down for yourself. Place them on your wall.

Health

#49. Think this: Eat organic food. Not that: Don't eat synthetic-chemical food that comes from modern farming.

Our food system is just plain crazy. Now, before you call me a tree-hugging, tofu-eating, Birkenstock-wearing trouble maker, it should be noted I was a burger-eating, football-watching, trouble maker (for the record, I don't like tofu, and you'll never see me in a pair of Birkenstocks). Then I read Michael Pollan's *The Omnivore's Dilemma* and my world was shaken to its core. Here's an excerpt from the book:

When humankind acquired the power to fix nitrogen [through the use of chemical fertilizers, a process discovered by an ex-Nazi chemical-weapons inventor], the basis of soil fertility shifted from a total reliance on the energy of the sun to a new reliance on fossil fuel...every bushel of industrial corn requires the equivalent of between a quarter and a third of a gallon of oil to grow it, or around 50 gallons of oil per acre of corn...it takes more than a calorie of fossil-fuel energy to produce a calorie of food; before the advent of chemical fertilizer, the farm produced more than two calories of food energy for every calorie of energy invested....

Pollan also talks about how this excess nitrogen has caused algae to bloom in rivers and ocean "dead zones," in which fish cannot live, and says, "By fertilizing the world, we alter the planet's composition and shrink its biodiversity."

I still watch football, but I quit eating standard, farm-raised beef because cattle are fed corn to fatten them up quickly, but they are not designed to eat it, so it leads to infections. They are then given antibiotics, which make their way up the food chain to us, so that when we need to take an antibiotic, it doesn't work for us anymore.

Corn is also made into high-fructose corn syrup, which sweetens soft drinks and is included in many processed foods, because it is much cheaper than sugar. Scientists suspect that since HFCS is not a natural food, it is not "recognized" by the body and thus brings us only calories, while none of the nutrition from the corn is absorbed. Drinking soft drinks and eating processed foods made with HFCS may be one of the main reasons for the Type II diabetes epidemic in the U.S.

Once I became aware of this food challenge for myself, I started paying attention to what kind of food that people were donating to the shelter. It was nutty. Frozen chicken nuggets. White bread. White sugar. High fat canned food. Cheap food. You get the picture.

People who come into the shelter already have compromised health and immune systems because of the stress of the homeless lifestyle choices as well as prior drug and alcohol addiction. Now, combine that with high-fat, low-nutrition food that is basically deadly even to the most healthy of people. It was like putting a match to dynamite.

Heard enough? Even if you don't consider yourself an organic food type, you can't help but wonder if putting hundreds if not thousands of pounds of pesticides, arsenic and other unnamed chemicals in your food to help them grow has an effect on your body. I could go on for days, but I won't.

Now here's the good news.

Nutritionist Maria Rodale does spectacular investigative in her book *Organic Manifesto* by elaborating on what happens when you switch to eating organic foods:

Your immune system will benefit. University of Colorado Neuroscientist Christopher Lowry found that certain strains of soil-borne bacteria that are killed by the pesticides actually help stimulate the immune system.

You'll help stop global warming (whether you believe it or not). Mycorrhizal fungi in the soil absorbs and neutralizes carbon. When we sterilize the soil through chemicals, we kill this naturally occurring carbon checker. More carbon, more global warming.

We'll be able to feed more people in the world. Despite the propaganda, modern organic farming is just as effective in producing mass as chemically produced product. Even more, organic farming will keep other countries from soil degradation by using chemicals. More usable soil, more food.

You'll get more nutrients, thus become healthier. A 2007 study from the University of California at Davis shows that some organic foods have more disease-fighting antioxidants than chemically-farmed foods. Even if you're nutrient conscious, you're getting short changed unless your food is certified organic.

And based on my experience I have to say, organic wines taste better. Something about leaving out the sulfites allows more of the fruitiness to come through. That's not necessarily a rigorous scientific study, just my personal observation. And I'd like to think of myself as a connoisseur.

If there is a no-brainer in the world, switching from eating the crap that's being provided through contemporary farming to eating organic and natural foods has to be it.

#50. Think this: Food Consciousness changes the way we eat. Not that: Weight Loss Dieting helps you lose weight.

Obesity and poverty usually go hand in hand. Many of my students who came from poverty environments battle weight problems. But in the United States, obesity spreads across the socioeconomic playing field. The country is fat overall, so dieting is as common as brushing your teeth— everybody's doing it because it's necessary.

As most of us have figured out, dieting doesn't work—at least, not in the long run. With this in mind, I talk about weight loss from a food consciousness perspective. I ask my students about the relationship they have with food. Are you fighting with food? Do you have a love/hate relationship with it? Is food your friend or your enabler? When was the last time you and food clearly defined your relationship? All of these questions become part of our food consciousness approach. Food consciousness is more productive than diet simply because it provides some basic benefits:

1. A change in unconscious food consumption.

2. A way to reduce costs in health maintenance expenditure.

3. A focus on quality of life.

4. A way to deal with the source of poor health (an unhealthy lifestyle) instead of the symptoms (weight gain).

A healthy lifestyle that includes regular exercise, reducing sedentary habits along with better food simply makes more sense that one-time diets. Anyone who has ever done special, temporary diets knows that the weight lost almost always comes back with a vengeance. As it returns, it becomes harder to lose the next time around. Part of that is not just about will power, but about how modern food is processed. Dr.Gene-Jack Wang, chair of the medical department at the U.S. Department of Energy's Brookhaven National Laboratory, says, "We make our food very similar to cocaine now." Coca leaves have been used since ancient times, he points out, but people learned to purify or alter cocaine to deliver it more efficiently to their brains (by injecting or smoking it, for instance). This made the drug more addictive. According to Wang, food has evolved in a similar way. "We purify our food," he says. "Our ancestors ate whole grains, but we're eating white bread. American Indians ate corn; we eat corn syrup." The ingredients in purified modern food cause people to "eat unconsciously and unnecessarily," and will also prompt an animal to "eat like a drug abuser " says Wang.

Once I started sharing this information from Dr. Wang, students in my class who struggled through substance abuse were able to relate more directly and started to think about their eating habits.

Developing food consciousness means that, even if we can't afford organic or natural foods, we can at least pay more attention to everything that goes in our mouths and can make decisions on frequency and amount. For my students, it is a start.

#51. Think this: Just Say No (to prescription drugs). Not that: The bigger the headache, the bigger the pill.

So many of my students had been recovering from substance abuse I felt it was necessary for us to talk about drugs, not just the illegal kind.

In some ways, Nancy Reagan was ahead of her time. Her plea to get more young people to stay away from trying illegal drugs by just saying "no" was memorable. But in the 21st century, particularly in the United States, the "just say no" plea is more about prescription drugs and saying no to an unhealthy lifestyle. It's not your imagination if you're hearing more people talk about preventative health care by losing weight, exercising daily, eating better food and slowing down your world. The very fast-paced, indulgent life that we've worked hard to obtain is now killing us at an alarming rate. Unfortunately, our push is to get a pill to fix the problem. But in the words of Dr. TE Holt, from his powerful article in *Men's Health Magazine*, "Few problems are so simple that they can be solved with a pill: few drugs are so simple that they don't cause problems of their own".

You might have heard your mother say something like that years ago. Now the data, the medical establishment and the health community are making your mother out to be a sage. Despite the authoritative and medical look of those intense and powerful ads by the pharmaceutical companies, they are selling a product – drugs- and seeking to make money on that product by presenting it to the largest consumer market they can find. The idea that many of the medical challenges we face can be dealt with through preventative care and lifestyle choices before filling that prescription is not exactly what the companies want to hear. That would cut into their profit margin. And this drug-first lifestyle idea has support. At this writing, the United States has been mired in a health care system that basically rewards pill-taking hypochondria more than healthy, active, thoughtful living. Fortunately, President Obama's new health care bill may help to change this level of institutional madness. If anything, it helped us take a look at something many of us have suspected for a long time—our health care system is a mess.

Don't get me twisted on this—some things can only be dealt with through a drug and medical care regimen. Some things discovered and developed by the pharmaceutical companies are nothing short of miraculous. But, as in all things, it is possible that we've swung the pendulum too far to one side. The new conventional wisdom of "just say no to prescription drugs" is trying to bring us back to something that looks more balanced and sane. That's real talk.

#52. Think this: Eat all day long. Not that: Eat three big square meals a day.

Part of the mission of the class is to get students to ask questions about their lifestyle, and not just the more obvious ones that seem destructive. We talk to them about getting more than 6 hours of sleep to help their concentration during the day; engaging in a regular program of meditation to help manage stress; changing up the way they eat to manage their weight and health

That means smaller meals spread throughout the day.

This may sound a little counterintuitive to those seeking to lose weight. Eating all day long makes you sound like a pig at a trough, but just the opposite is true. When we regulate our eating only to three big meals a day, we tend to overeat and not allow our bodies the opportunity to fully digest the food we stuff in our faces. That food can get stored as fat as the body seeks to save that food for a rainy day. Eating smaller meals throughout the day—or even three smaller meals—keeps us from wolfing down at these appointed times—morning, noon and night. In farming cultures years ago, three square meals were the mainstay because working in the fields burned off a lot of calories. Now that most of the world lives in major cities doing less laborious work, we need to adjust our eating process accordingly.

There is much controversy surrounding how many of these meals we should eat. Some say six small ones, others argue that three square smaller ones would do the trick too. Everything that I've read to date says eating smaller and throughout the day to prevent hunger is the key. The most important goal is to prevent you from getting hungry. When we are hungry, we tend to overeat. If you are eating smaller, low fat, low-carb meals throughout the day, you avoid the "hungry binge." The students at the shelter are on a fixed meal schedule, but I am petitioning management to see if we can change up the three meals structure and still make it cost effective for them to "graze" all day long,

#53. Think this: Drink water when you're thirsty. Not that: You should drink eight, 8-ounce glasses of water a day.

One of the health care workers at the shelter did a presentation in one of my classes to remind the students to drink eight 8 ounces of glasses of water a day. One of my students said "That's hard for me to think about drinking that much water each day." That drove me to see if we can find another way of helping the students drink more water without making it an arduous task. I discovered that the eight glasses of water a day was an unsubstantiated conventional wisdom. At least, that's what the experts were saying.

In typical conventional wisdom form, this urban legend moved from unverified concept to widely accepted truism at the blink of an eye. As with most myths, they are based in fact...then they stray. To remain healthy adults, we need to take in enough water to replace that which we've lost due to sweating, excretion, and just breathing. Of course, if you're like me and you have a regular 3- to 4-day-a-week workout schedule, salsa dance two or three nights a week and hike, you'll need to drink more water than the guy whose life is more sedentary. Even the idea that if you don't drink this amount of water each day will cause you to be dehydrated is a false notion. "The concept that there is widespread dehydration among populations of people that don't drink eight 8 ounce glasses of water each day has not basis in medical fact."

Those are the words of Dr. Robert Alpern, dean of the medical school at the University of Texas Medical Center.

The general consensus in the medical community is that you should drink when you're thirsty. If you don't feel thirsty, don't drink unless you want to. This conventional wisdom repeal should be welcome news for a lot of you who felt frustrated with those frequent journeys to the bathroom trying to maintain your 8-glass regimen.

#54. Think this: There is such a thing as a good death. Not that: Death is bad.

A dear friend of mine died of cancer during the writing of this book. I was one of the volunteer hospice support workers during the 6 months she struggled on that journey between a miracle healing and preparation for passing. There were days when we as care workers didn't quite know what road we were on until someone said we are on both roads. This is the space that Hospice workers walk every day. Their job is to help us embrace this part of the human journey so that whatever the outcome, we are prepared and that we do it well.

For a long time, anything dealing with death was seen as inappropriate conversation for mixed company. Seeing death as "the enemy" and not talking about it was (and still is) the standard approach for many. The only time most people in Western countries even had the conversation was through their life insurance programs. Hospice care allows us to dig deeper into developing protocol around this life phase with courage, dignity, peacefulness, preparedness, awareness, adjustment, acceptance and a program. This is called The Good Death movement.

The Good Death movement is centered around our being open and honest about death, about making sure the person who knows of their limited time live out his/her remaining days in dignity, and creating ceremony that the person passing, their friends, family and loved ones can participate in while that person is still here.

We often talk about death in the class, simply because so many of my students are dealing with thoughts of suicide. A student who did share his suicide thoughts out loud with the rest of the class said killing himself would be a form of Good Death because he'll die on his own terms. First, I commended him for his honesty and courage to talk about this subject out loud. Then I brought his attention to his death plans and posed the following questions:

- "I wonder what would happen if you put as much thought into your life as you would your death?
- What would happen if you have a good life plan?
- "What's the rush?"
- "You're going to miss the Cubs win the World Series!"

That last one had him and the rest of the class busted out in laughter and eased some of the tension. He then opened up and talked more openly about his personal frustrations.

This round of questioning helped us not to undercut the importance of the Good Death movement and the importance of talking about the subject, but to compliment it with our living experience so that both could be an affirming experience as much as we can control.

You'll probably start hearing more people use the term The Good Death in more ways than a euphemism. It is becoming a way we start to plan our end of life events.

#55. Think this: Eating too much will make you gain weight. Not that: Eating right before you go to bed will make you gain weight.

Weight and personal health care is always a hot topic in the class because so many people are batting health and weight challenges. One of the students asked me about eating at night because he always felt hungry right before he went to bed. It was a very difficult challenge for him, so I decided to look into what the science said about it.

If you eat a king's banquet right before you go to bed, yes, you will gain weight. But if you eat a king's banquet pretty regularly, whether it's at night, in the morning or in the middle of the day, you're going to pack on the pounds. The point is that eating right before you go to bed, by itself, will not make you gain weight, but eating too much will. Study after study, some of which have been printed in the *British Medical Journal*, continually prove eating at night, or any particular time of the day, won't make you fat.

Part of the reason why we single out eating at night as a weight gain villain is that we believe if we're up and about, we can burn off what we eat. However, if you eat too much, the body, whether active or inactive, will store that extra food as fat and save it just in case you're in a starvation situation. In most industrialized countries, few of us are in starvation situations, so we just end up carrying that storage.

So go on and have that extra drumstick or bowl of ice cream while you're in the bed watching your *Law and Order* reruns you missed. Just have smaller servings.

#56. Think this: Your body is your primary care physician. Not that: Your doctor is your primary care physician.

A few months back, I pinched a nerve in my middle back, probably due to a pretty aggressive weight training program I took up after I returned from overseas. I thought I would make up for the time I had off. Of course, that was foolish of me. It was one of the most painful injuries I could remember. I went online and the best sites were all saying the same things: "You've got a pinched nerve. Ice down your back, get some massage, ramp up your meditation practice (if you have one) and leave the rest to your body. It knows what to do."

Sure enough, my body did exactly what it was designed to do—self repair and self heal. I noticed that many of my students don't trust their bodies anymore. They feel that it has betrayed them and that the health challenges they suffer is because the body had become their enemy.

While it is true that for many of us, our bodies seem to be doing things against our will, the body is also our best healer and doctor. Our challenge, like in any relationship, is that we don't treat our bodies right.

When we don't develop a relationship with our body

through better food, plenty of sleep and exercise, our body breaks down. Instead of going back to develop that relationship so that it's healthy, we tend to seek another lover, namely, the doctor. We figure that the doctor will work out what the body has failed to do. But the mark of a wise and insightful doctor is one that will tell you to go back and develop your relationship with your first love, your body. If she's a good doctor, she'll tell you to "rest /and let your body do the work".

In many Western societies, we've developed conventional wisdom that focuses on "experts." We believe there are professionals who could work miracles above and beyond what we could do ourselves. Sure, for that 1–5% of the catastrophic things that happen in our lives, it's good to have an expert surgeon. But for the rest of the 95% of our health challenges, the body is expert. The reason we're seeing the explosion of health magazines is because more people understand that doctors simply can't do it all. There are things we can do to cultivate healing in ourselves.

The real challenge we face is having compromised immune deficiencies due to poor nutrition and lack of self-care. This ties one hand and one leg behind the back of our bodies as it tries to do its work. Our job is to give our bodies everything it needs to do it's job right—good food, regular exercise and healthy living.

#57. Think this: Laughter allows us to process better. Not that: This is not the time for fun and games.

I can be as stern as the next guy, but I know that when I infuse self-effacing humor and keep my class laughing, they seemed to receive the lesson much more willingly. From talking about my dating misadventures, to my confessions of a not-so-perfect Dad, to the days when I didn't have two dimes to rub together, I told many a humorous story, to the delight of my students.

Psychologist Dr. Paul McGhee says that humor has a powerful way of directly improving our overall health. He says, for the past 25 years, there has been a tremendous growth in the "humor and health" movement, where physicians are realizing the power of humor in our healing process—both physically and mentally. Here are some other things attributed directly to humor:

1. It increases the body's production of endorphins, thus relieving some pain.
2. It binds groups together in commonality, reducing stress from separateness.
3. It relaxes certain muscle groups that would not otherwise relax.
4. It allows a level of temporary escape from frustration.
5. Laughter creates group support.

I won't give up my day job for a Comedy Works tour, but I do appreciate the power of simple basic humor when working with those in the most challenging situations.

#58. Think this: Be aware of the Don King effect. Not that: We're right. They're wrong.

Boxing impresario, iconic figure and flamboyant personality Don King is a master at his craft. It's not just his hair style that brought him to fame. It's his ability to create and promote a fight. He makes his millions by instigating a conflict between boxers, then finding financing to promote the fight.

Anytime there is conflict between individuals, political parties, groups of people or even countries, it's because there is a Don King hanging around somewhere. This person or persons is instigating the conflict, financing it, and finding ways to keep it going because they're making money on it. From arms dealers to divorce lawyers to talk show hosts to funeral parlors to shadowy quasi-governmental figures, someone is benefiting from conflict. A resolution or compromise would short-change their income flow. The unfortunate people in the conflict often don't even know it's going on. All they want is to be right and to win. But in most long-term, on-going conflicts, the only winner is the Don King figure.

My students were regularly engaged in long-term conflicts with spouses and relatives. In fact, many of them became homeless because of their desire to "win" the conflict at all costs. By asking a few more questions, I found that there usually was some third party that benefited from my student being in conflict, whether it was a relative that didn't want them back, a case worker who could use the conflict as job leverage, or a divorce lawyer who cleaned up. We spent some time talking about the Don King effect and how not to become perpetual conflict addicts. We now use a three-step questioning process whenever conflicts arise. The questions are:

1. Do you want to be right or effective?
2. Who stands to gain the most from your conflict?
3. What would happen if you let it go?

If you find yourself in conflict against an intractable opponent, ask these questions for yourself, and then opt out of the game so that you're no longer being 'played.'

5 *Shift Tool* **Creating Your Affirmations.**

As a former advertising copywriter, I've learned the power of words and have utilized some of those words in ad campaigns. If you want to give yourself an idea and make it part of your thinking, you have to regularly and consistently present that idea to yourself in the form of an affirmation. Here are some tools for best utilizing affirmation statements:

1. Always write in the present. For personal affirmation, you'll want to state what is, and not what you hope.

For example, if you want to be more courageous than you are now, your statement should state, "I am courageous," not "I want to be courageous." The latter statement only tells the mind of something it hopes for at some future date as opposed to what it is.

2. Tie your affirmation into a current pop culture phrase. Everyone is talking about things becoming "green" or "sustainable." Whenever you can, incorporate some of these popular words in your affirmation. For example, you can write a statement like "My business is a sustainable system that empowers me as well as those who work with me." Whenever the word "sustainable" comes up in popular culture, it will bring you back to remembrance of your affirmation. This is how you leverage pop culture to your advantage.

3. Focus on a desired outcome. What's wrong with this affirmation?: "I don't want to be overweight any more." That's not an affirmation. That's a hope and maybe a prayer. Affirmations simply state a desired outcome as though it already is. It certainly is no guarantee of the outcome, but it can increase the odds of your success for that desired outcome simply by getting you to think about it more often.

4. Use effective words in your affirmations. In advertising, we have a mental list of words that tend to work more effective in getting people to remember things than others. In fact, the psychology

department at Yale University has identified 10 of the most powerful words in our media-based society. They are: new, save, you, safety, proven, love, discover, guarantee, health and save.

5. Get to the point. Your affirmations don't have to be gigantic discourses on your deeper inner feelings. Get to the point. Keep the affirmation in a sentence or two so that it's easy to remember.

Politics

#59. Think this: We need an Evolution. Not that: We need a Revolution.

Political romantics often speak of needing a revolution to change the status quo. This highly-charged word makes governments paranoid, housewives want to put away the silver, and student organizations nutty. In my understanding, revolution would be the same as shuffling the deck chairs on the *Titanic*. You're moving things around, but the boat is still sinking. The very nature of the word "revolution" means that there is a revolving circle happening, where I am on top one day and you're on the bottom. As the cycle revolves, you're on top and I'm on the bottom. And so it goes. That's okay if the system works. Everybody gets a chance to play Top Dog at some point. But if the system is broken, revolution is a waste of time.

What's becoming clear is the new word of choice, "evolution." Evolution doesn't throw out the baby with the bath water when it comes to change. It seeks to take that which is and build a new process on top of it. The power of evolution is that you get the chance to incorporate newer ideas that may be needed for the time. When organizations are not flexible enough to evolve, they leave the door open for revolutions which become angry, desperate affairs.

Violence occurs with people jockeying for position in a burning house.

Evolution allows a natural confluence of ideas that can lead to something great happening. Of course, this kind of change is often feared because many believe it will mean an end to that which they know as familiar. However, the nature of evolution is to build upon that which is while introducing newer, necessary ideas for the organism to continue existing.

This principle is critical when working with people in transition. We do an exercise where the student shares what things they've learned from being homeless because yes, there are things to learn being homeless, if you pay attention. From there, we talk about how we would leverage this new information into wisdom going forward. This is important because often, people who go through really tough situations don't want to remember the event. They just want to move on. But I know that we need to recover the old stuff so that we can extract the wisdom, then build a new "house" upon that wisdom. It's the evolutionary process at work.

My belief is that we're at a crossroads as human beings. Faced with climate change, shrinking resources due to waste and exploitation, ideas that enslave instead of empower, we are being asked to move above and beyond that we know. We could continue the cycle that we're in and hope that we end up with a chair when the musical chairs song stops playing. Or we can leave that game and opt for something more sustainable, more flexible, more inclusive and more empowering.

I admit, this is my editorial, but it's based on diligent observation.

#60. Think this: We need Leadership. Not that: We need better Leaders.

I was in Namibia recently and conducted a seminar on personal empowerment to a packed house of unemployed young adults. In the discussion, the constant enemy was the government leaders and what they were not doing for the people. So I asked: "Now that we know what the leaders are not doing, what are you going to do?" The idea that there was something they could do outside of the wishes of the leaders seemed strangely foreign to the attendees. They constantly wanted to go back to what the leaders weren't doing and I constantly steered them back to the question "what are you going to do about it?"

After several hours of this, I realized the biggest challenge to these young adults, and perhaps to the people of Namibia was their ability to define Leadership. Leadership and leaders are not necessarily the same thing. Leaders, as I define it, are the people sent by the Leadership (the people) to exercise their will. From the attendees' perspective, the Leaders were the people chosen to take care and make decisions for the rest of us. This not-so-subtle shift in understanding is starting to take hold around the world.

In this new definition of leadership, we need to provide more clarity about what is leadership. Protest is not leadership. Complaining is not leadership. Having a talk show is not leadership. Protest is part of the process, but it is not leadership. Anybody and everybody can get up and gripe about stuff, but leaders are the people who take the next courageous step and actually offer a plan and affirmative hope for the people.

The days of the God/King complex, where leaders were seen as divine or "chosen" is giving way to democracy movements. Maybe not Democracy in the way the West defines it, but definitely a form that gives voice to the people.

#61. Think this: We need a campaign for something. Not that: We need a War On Terror, Drugs, Poverty, etc.

Maybe it's the use of the word "war." Maybe it's because the ideas aren't well conceived. Maybe it's because some of the efforts are highly politicized. Whatever the case, the highly public and highly financed "wars" in the U.S. have been anything but victorious. The Great Society's War On Poverty has only seen continued socioeconomic stratification. The War On Drugs is probably one of the worst public policies ever devised. The War On Terror is an open-ended task with no specific enemy, no defined way to gauge victory and no end in sight.

What these efforts have in common is our previous obsession with the idea that a war can resolve our problems. The belief is that if we commit enough money and resources, we can lick the problem. Only now are we noticing the limits of throwing money at a problem without thinking it through. Oddly enough, our most cost-effective accomplishments have been campaigns that raised awareness and relied on peer support: wearing seat belts, not driving drunk, and not smoking. These were not called "The War Against Not Wearing Seatbelts" or "The War Against Smoking" or the "War Against Drunk Driving." They were awareness campaigns that emphasized personal responsibility. Check out these comparisons:

- The War On Drugs focuses on stopping the supply side of the drug business as opposed to focusing on the demand side.

- The Reduce Drunk Driving campaign emphasized what we individually could do to reduce the problem (Friends don't let friends drive drunk). The push was NOT against the alcohol industry.

- The War On Poverty focused on having government resolve the problem for the people. It forgot to ask the people how to get the problem resolved.

- The Campaign on wearing seat belts didn't go after car makers to make better seat belts, but warned us to individually act ("Click it or ticket").

It seems that when we take personal ownership of the challenge out of the equation, our success rate suffers.

Social scientists and policy makers are now noticing this difference. Steve Flynn, President of the Center for National Policy in Washington DC, says this of the War on Terror: "Washington should ask citizens to share the responsibility for preparing the nation to cope with the man-made and natural disasters by funding Citizens Corps programs. When individuals and communities are better able to withstand, recover and adapt to catastrophic risks, terrorism will become more like the common cold: a new strain may emerge each season, but it will have little effect on the nation's daily life".

That would, in effect, end the main goal of terrorism—to immobilize the public into fear, panic and paralysis.

Using this knowledge, I started approaching students about creating their own "campaigns" for their lives. Instead of saying things like, "I don't want to be poor," I help them develop their own "I am ____" campaign. It helps them incorporate personal responsibility, develop an action plan with specific goals, and it gives them a more positive approach to old problems. Some students go as far as to create posters and slogans for their campaign, making it more personal and tangible. The student's campaign "for" something seems to work quite well. My suspicion is that the constant drumbeat of being against something without a break is too negative over an extended period of time. Being for something gave the students a proactive direction.

People need to feel there is something they can do.

#62. Think this: World peace is actually achievable. Not that: War is a necessary evil.

When dealing with people going through transition, the most important thing you can do is bring hope and optimism. In fact, I'll say it's an absolute necessity. You're talking to people who have spent years in very dark places. Just a little bit of hope can go a long way.

But bringing hope can't be a rose-colored, feel-good pep rally. You have to show real world, actual possibilities so students can see themselves in the example or see the example as credible. If you don't, you'll lose credibility as a teacher. People in transition are a tough crowd. You don't BS them with glittering generalities. I went way out and decided to talk to my students about war.

I know, I know. Just stay with me on this one. Much to the chagrin of my end times religious friends who remind me that "wars and rumors of wars" is a sure sign of the apocalypse, there are fewer wars in the world today. Not only are they fewer but since the bloody turn of the 19th/20th century, war as a tool to solve problems has been trending downward, rather dramatically. Yep, it's true.

Make no mistake, there ARE wars in the world as we speak—the Afghanistan conflict, Palestine, Sudan, Burundi, Somalia—and let's not forget about Columbia. But the onetime regular tool of traditional war—fought between two, uniformed, state-sponsored armies—is on the way out. The news gets better. Not only are the big nasty fights that defined World Wars I and II gone, but also there has been a significant decrease in the number of civil wars in countries around the world since the early 1990s. This is the news coming from a number of organizations that pay attention to these kinds of things, including the prestigious University of Uppsala Conflict Data Program in Sweden.

What we have left are the vestiges of war-like behavior—guerrilla campaigns, insurgencies and terrorism. But then, even terrorism has been trending down, despite the popular media feeds that would make you believe just the opposite. Acts of terrorism have been trending downward since the height of bombings against people in the mid 1980s. During this period of time, the Jewish Defense League, Eco Terrorists and the Colombian Popular Liberation Army were active and deadly. While there were more people killed in the 9/11 tragedy, the trend of terrorist acts have been dwindling significantly. These are the latest findings from the FBI National Counterterrorism Center.

Another clear sign that war doesn't have the same power in our lives that it used to: fewer people are dying. According to researcher Milton Leitenberg of the University of Maryland, from 1900 through 1950 over 3.8 million people were killed each year because of wars and conflicts. In 2008, 25,600 people were killed (both soldiers and civilians) total. Not only are there fewer conflicts, they kill fewer people.

Of course, all of this is cold comfort for those who have suffered under the cloud of armed conflict, but make no mistake—there is a change in the way humankind looks at armed conflict, and it bodes well for the dream of world peace that seemed virtually impossible just a few years ago.

How did this dramatic development escape us? Why are we not dancing in the streets?

One of my journalism school profs used to remind me of a basic truth about the human condition: we are instinctively wired to seek out and pay attention to threats to our survival. Call it a gift from our early days on the plains of Africa, but this survival technique helped us escape the saber-tooth tiger and all of the other dangers that threatened our very existence as a species. We still have that programming. So while there may be news about wonderful developments happening around the world, we only pay attention to the ones we perceive as a threat. There is a reason why doomsday talk show hosts do so well—as long as they wrap their rhetoric in threats to your survival and your way of life, your instinctive brain sees that information in the same way it sees a Saber-tooth tiger, thus the guy who talks about your country going to hell in a hand basket is going to get more attention than the guy who talks about the great things that are happening. The doomsday people have a genetic advantage on their side. Once I told this to my students, it allowed them to take another look at possibilities they couldn't see before because it was obscured by their pessimism.

When peace activists, beauty-pageant contestants and little children talk about world peace, it used to seem more like a hope than a possibility. Now, the numbers show that possibility is within our reach.

I am not so naïve as to believe there will not be wars in our future. What I'm saying is that the data is giving us evidence to know that wars are not necessary. People have to choose war.

#63. Think this: Slouching when you're sitting is okay. Not that: Sit upright in your chair or you'll have bad posture.

Why not talk about slouching? Many of my clients were working on their posture and their slouching so I indulged them. My emphasis on this made me discover something new in my research.

We've been told by our Moms to sit up straight in our chairs, or we'll have terrible posture, ruined spines, get hunchback syndrome and every other thing our Mothers could think of. And for the most part (with the exception of us reprobate writers who spend long hours in front of a computer) their scare tactics worked. Now for the new conventional wisdom. Slouching is okay.

Researchers at Woodend Hospital in Aberdeen, Scotland using a new form of magnetic resonance imaging (MRI) discovered that sitting in an upright position places unnecessary strain on your back, leading to potentially chronic pain problems if you spend long hours sitting. "We were not created to sit down for long hours, but somehow modern life requires the vast majority of the global population to work in a seated position," said Dr. Waseem Amir Bashir who authored the study.

Despite the evidence in this study, I will probably go back to sitting in an upright, 90-degree position when I return home for Thanksgiving, per my mother's request. Otherwise, I'll be banished to the kid's table.

#64. Think this: Africa is the next major engine of economic growth in the world. Not that: Africa is a poor continent plagued by trouble and needs our help.

I remember coming back from one of my South Africa teaching trips at the University of Kwazulu-Natal in Durban, and one of my students asked me if I saw lions running through the streets. I started to laugh until I looked at the student's face and realized she was serious. She, and others in the class, had this cartoon concept and idea of Africa they picked up from popular media. So, we started having days when we would simply talk about world affairs. Most of these students had no clue about things in the rest of the world, nor did they care. They figured the only thing they needed to be concerned about was whether or not they had a roof over their head that night. I made a strong argument that what our country does in the world has an indirect if not direct affect on that roof because of our connectedness. That's when I went into detail about Africa and our relationship with it.

The worldwide accounting/professional-services firm KPMG came out in 2010 with a definitive statement about the African continent. It says Africa is the next great frontier when it comes to growth in the world. They cite numerous factors that are already in place. It is the richest continent on the earth when it comes to minerals. It has a relatively low population in relation to its size. Its population is the youngest on earth. It is strategically positioned between Europe, the East and the Middle East. And, one of the things I've noticed from my travels in the continent—young Africans have a distinct hunger for higher education. China has already discovered these truths and has become the continent's biggest trade partner over the past 10 years.

KPMG goes on to say that Western conventional wisdom may obscure the point that Africa is for trade, not just aid. Countries that see the continent as a trading partner will have access to the great resources Africa has to offer. In exchange, African infrastructure, education, health and transportation systems will be greatly updated to eventually help the continent leapfrog into the future.

Why does the "help poor Africa" narrative persist? It's not that the continent doesn't have its share of challenges. That's an understatement. It's just that those citing poor Africa have lost historical perspective. Africa on whole has only relatively recently broken from the chains of colonization. We're talking no more than 60 full years of freedom. In contrast, it took hundreds of years for Western Europe to break out of its social and economic deterioration due to barbaric in-fighting, decline in populations, collapse in economic trade and perpetual plagues—all of this following the fall of the Western Roman Empire. This period in Europe is commonly known as the Dark Ages. By comparison, Africa is transitioning out of its period of outside control at breakneck speed. Even China, at one time regarded as a Third World country filled with internal strife, took eons to become the power it is today. Not until the 1970s did the West look at anything coming out of Asia as having quality. "Made in China" was a point of ridicule. Now, China is becoming the next superpower.

My, how things change.

I challenge my students to know more about their world and not rely upon a fairly inconsistent domestic news media. I tell them that the beginning of seeing themselves differently starts with seeing their world from a higher perch. This gives you perspective. From that perch, you should be able to get a pretty good view of Africa, too.

#65. Think this: What works is localization. Not that: What works is globalization.

One of the challenges we have at the shelter is that it's hard to keep volunteers over an extended period of time. The volunteer arrives, stays for a few weeks, then we'd never see him/her again. When I asked some people about doing volunteer work there, many of them responded by telling me about the donations they were making to global causes. That's cool, but there's something to be said about charity beginning at home. If you want to change the way the world is going, do something in your backyard. The localization movement gets this. Even in the face of increased globalization.

Let me offer some clarification. Globalization will not disappear in the face of localization. It's just that localization is becoming a major focal point for communities, cities and states everywhere in response to globalization. In many countries, both Conservatives and Progressives alike will find this a place they can find common ground. Localization is the emphasis on the primacy of local products and services and duty in a 50-mile radius of where you live. You're already hearing phrases that speak to this new conventional wisdom: Locavores, Local Yokalls, Locally Sourced. Something that comes from a place within 50 miles of where you live will start to take on special value as localization continues to spread.

What will probably happen is something of a hybrid world, where you'll be transferring funds from your Canadian-based bank through your smart phone, as you prepare to make a purchase from the Farmer's Market just down the street from your home right before you volunteer at the local homeless shelter.

It's a brave new world. Do something close to home.

#66. Think this: It's good to check stuff out. Not that: Conspiracy Theories are wacky ideas by people who need to get a life.

The first time I meet my students, I tell them several things they should know about me before they listen to anything I say:

1. I am a volunteer, so I am not paid by the Catholic Archdiocese that runs the Samaritan house.
2. I am not an agent of any particular religious organization.
3. I am not a Pastor or theologian.
4. I am not here to settle a work release or community service score.
5. I am not undercover for the NSA, FBI, CIA, DHS, NBA, NFL, KKK, PTA or the WWE.

I finish by suggesting that the students Google me to help fill in some of the gaps. From the many papers I've submitted to different conferences around the world, to my website and reviews of my books, they'll get a better composite of who I am and what I represent.

I emphasize to the students the importance of checking people out who come to speak to them. It's good to check stuff out. That applies also to the many conspiracy theories that are all over the place.

Homeless shelters are packed with people sharing conspiracy theories. These theories sometimes act as substitutions for knowledge because they are quick, simple and often fully developed so the listener doesn't have to do any work to embrace it. I suggest that not checking out conspiracy theories, then embracing them immediately lowers your quality of life because you start living your world through someone else's fears. That immediately takes away possibilities that you may have otherwise pursued. I actually heard a student justify why he was not going to apply for a particular government job because, in his words, "The government's a fascist regime anyway."

I found out later he didn't apply for the job because he had a felony on his record.

Whether you have a felony or not, check stuff out. Judge for yourself what theories are true and what are not. Don't rely on talk-show hosts or a frustrated friend to give you clarity. They can't. They have their own issues to work out.

And remember, just because someone calls it a conspiracy theory doesn't necessarily mean it's a theory.

6 The Kinfolk Test

One of my mentors in advertising told me that if I could not explain my idea to my grandmother in a sentence or two where she could say, "Okay, got it," I was either a liar, a fool or a politician (or all of the above). He told me that powerful ideas cut through, are memorable and relatively simple to the intellect. This is similar to Michael

Pollan's rule in his book *The Omnivore's Dilemma*. He says if you're about to put something in your mouth that your grandmother does not recognize as food, it's probably not.

Want to get some clarity on an idea that you're not sure about? Run it by your grandparents.

Society

#67. Think this: We really are all the same. Not that: We are all different races of people.

Repeat after me: there is no such thing as race. There is no such thing as race. There is no such thing as race.

Part of our ritual for the class I teach is that everyone has to get up and tell the story of how they ended up at the shelter. Every once in a while, a conflict would erupt in the class when an African-American student blamed his challenges on white people and when a white student blamed the problems of the world on African Americans. They both were looking for someone to blame in the middle of their troubles, so they resurrected race as a convenient scapegoat. They both were seeking to construct a referendum on race when the 800-pound gorilla in the room was class. So to take the bite out of the race trap, I broke off some pretty convincing science. There is no such thing as race.

The Human Genome Project basically put the race myth to bed. The final conclusion of the HGP was that all of us really are the same creature. Save the basic superficial differences of skin color, eye color and hair, we are genetically the same. We don't have to hold hands and

145

sing *Kumbaya* to convince people of this utopian idea—the science bears out the facts. The only humans that seem to be different than the rest of us are that group of 90,000 black people in Southern Africa called the San people, sometimes derisively known as Bushmen. They have significantly wider genetic diversity than all other human beings on earth put together, which led scientists to come to the conclusion that they are our living ancestors. I was so excited about this fact, I went to go visit them personally on the Kalahari in Namibia earlier this year, just so that I can say I touched a living ancestor. It was one of those things on my bucket list.

There's also the story of Henrietta Lacks, the African American woman, whose DNA was used back in the 1950s to create the HeLa strain ("He" for Henrietta and "La" for Lacks). This DNA strain is the source for which almost all of our major medical breakthroughs came from over the past 70 years. Had the doctors of that time subscribed to the idea that her DNA was "inferior" to white DNA, the rest of us would have never benefitted from the gift she gave us.

I constantly remind my students just because race doesn't exist doesn't mean there aren't people who seek to play it as a tool. There are those who discriminate based on the color of one's skin and those who leverage the issue as a way to seek political and power gains at the expense of people's willingness to believe. These are the people I call race-baiter. Next time you hear someone race-baiting, understand that it's a red herring designed to keep you from asking more important questions. It's a misdirection method, perpetrated by knuckleheads. Don't engage them. As my mother used to say, never fight with a fool, for passersby won't know the difference.

#68. Think this: Children should be seen and heard. Not that: Children should be seen and not heard.

Thanks to Oprah, most of us have figured out that a lot of our personal challenges stem from challenges in our past relationship with our parents. The more stories I hear from my students, the more I realize the root of their communication dysfunction: the old conventional wisdom that children are to be seen and not heard. Kids don't have any wisdom or knowledge to give. They should shut up and listen to their parents.

Believe it or not, a lot of people still hold to this idea, and may not even know they're doing it.

An enlightened society seeks ways of making sure their children are seen and heard. My folks were way ahead of the game by introducing Family Council meetings in the 1960s. We'd meet as a family once a week and talk about things we wanted to get done around the house and for us kids to have a voice in how things worked. We also had a chance to talk about school work and school stuff we were involved in. Not only were we ahead of most families, but we were virtually heretics in the African American community. Black families tended to adhere to a very strict top-down structure—no questions asked. I've always thought that was a cultural hold over from the hundreds of years of slave culture, where top-down discipline was the only game in town.

As with all things, there are extremes. I remember watching some of my white grade school colleagues talk to their parents with a level of aggressive disrespect that made me embarrassed as a fellow kid. It seemed that the parent was seeking to overcompensate for the "seen not heard" ideology, but they were only teaching their children how to disrespect other human beings (adults are human beings too). Everyone deserves respect and to be treated humanely. Allowing their children to treat them that way only means the rest of us are going to have to clean up the mess behind that kid when they become adults.

In the class, I helped the students rethink their communication relationship with their children for two reasons:

1. We need the practice.
2. Our children need to see it modeled.

Based on the crap I'm seeing down here on the ground, children not being part of our thought process earlier in life just leads to damage control later in life.

The "seen not heard" conventional wisdom is finally transitioning into a "all deserve to be heard" approach. What we're really saying to each other is that all of our thoughts and experiences are valued...no matter how old or young we are.

#69. Think this: Everyone needs to be media literate. Not that: Everyone needs to be reading literate.

I am fortunate enough to have as friends some of the finest video photographers, graphics artists and computer-generated film editors in the business. They are constantly showing me some of the newest and hottest software that allows them to create virtually anything you can imagine, digitally. Of course, this is great for Hollywood and entertainment in general, but what happens when people use those skills for evil instead of good? We'd have to be terribly naïve as to believe there aren't people with nefarious agendas who are seeing the power of video and film manipulation. And it doesn't have to be something so graphically powerful as to make us see unbelievable things. It could be as simple as editing a video out of context to make you believe a person is saying one thing, when, in context, they're saying something else.

We are in a media-based world. Shutting down media outlets, even the ones that manipulate our sense of what we see, isn't the answer. The answer is to develop media literacy. Media literacy is to the 21st Century what Literacy was to the 20th Century—without it, you could be left behind. Media literacy basically means helping the populace of a country understand the workings of a media-saturated world so that they become sophisticated enough to know what they see when they're seeing it. The EU is advancing this agenda with a series of studies to better understand how to educate its populace. One of their reports was the ground-breaking 2007 study, which states the four things need to be taught in schools:

1. The ability to keep private in a public place (such as what to say and what to post on Facebook, Twitter or MySpace).

2. The ability to prioritize, categorize and choose important data from a sea of data.

3. Having ethical and moral competencies when distributing information and interacting with other people.

4. Develop the ability to read and interpret data and images.

Not to teach media literacy to my students would mean not preparing them for basic survival in today's world. With that in mind, I developed a class around these four teaching points, kind of a "Going Online 101." The classes aren't elaborate, but students at least have an idea of what they deal with every time they're on the Net.

I am convinced that one of the true tools to personal success in the years ahead of us will be our ability to be prepared when we go online. The only defense against false information and more of an invasion to our privacy is being media literate.

#70. Think this: It's okay to say we just don't know. Not that: We know everything.

Many of my students cycle in homelessness because they are afraid of the future. Better the devil they know then the one they don't know. This observation led me to help my students from demonizing the unknown and start making friends with it.

The truth is that life is largely unpredictable and that we really don't know. Unfortunately, the power of our collective ego won't let us admit to that. This dilemma is well explained in Nassim Nicholas Taleb's book *The Black Swan*. His black swan theory basically says almost all major scientific discoveries, historical events, and artistic accomplishments are "black swans"—undirected and unpredicted. In other words, they were unknown. He identifies three criteria for black swan events:

1. The event is a surprise (to the observer).
2. The event has a major impact.
3. After the fact, the event is rationalized by hindsight, as if it had been expected.

It doesn't take a math whiz to realize this criteria basically describes most of the major events in our lifetime. From the birth of the internet to the 9/11 tragedy, the things that impacted our world the most we didn't see coming.

A similar idea is the "law of unintended consequences" (also called the "law of unforeseen consequences"), which states that any purposeful action will produce some unintended consequences. In other words, no action happens in a vacuum—it will often produce a initially intended consequence and one usually unanticipated by the person taking the action. Sociologist Thomas King Merton forwarded a more analytical approach to this idea. He states five principles of why unintended consequences can occur:

1. Ignorance—It is impossible to anticipate everything, despite a false belief that we can.

2. Error—We make an incorrect analysis of the situation.

3. Immediate interest—Our pressing needs can cause a change in how we respond to the intended outcome.

4. Basic beliefs—The filters in which we process information can cause us long term and habitual consequences to the action.

5. Self-fulfilling prophecy—Our beliefs will often drive us to find solutions before the problem occurs, thus the non-occurrence of the problem is unanticipated

We can ignore this truth and be in denial about it, or we can embrace the idea of being in the space of the unknown, allowing us to make room for the unexpected. It also helps us move out of a fear-based life and see new things that have been around us all along. Making peace in the space of the unknown can change everything.

Just sayin'….

#71. Think this: It's best to have experiences. Not that: It's best to have possessions.

Which would you choose—a day at the beach with loved ones or that new car?

A lot of my students would say "get the car" because you can use it well into the future, while a day at the beach is only for a moment. Of course, when you're in transition and are homeless, obtaining possessions becomes a preoccupation. Many of you would agree with them because we live in a consumer-based society. Value is usually based around how much and what kind of stuff you have. In order to keep my students from getting caught up in that maddening cycle, I bring them some emerging data that says experience has a greater pay off than possessions.

Leaf Van Boven, psychology professor at the University of Colorado at Boulder, gave students a national survey, which they used in five experiments to test their ideas.

In one of them, participants were told about people who had bought a material object or a life experience. Researches found that when the students learned about someone making a material purchase, this caused them to like that person less than a different person who purchased something experiential.

The authors concluded that people tend to have negative stereotypes about materialistic people. Participants asked to describe a materialistic person often used words such as "selfish" and "self-centered." When they described a experiential person, adjectives such as "altruistic," "friendly" and "outgoing" came up, the authors said.

Study co-author Thomas Gilovich, professor and chair of the psychology department at Cornell University, has pointed out in the past that comparing recent material purchases with friends generates more jealousy than trading stories about recent vacations. Material purchases can be compared physically—one person's television can be objectively bigger and brighter than her friend's—whereas each experience is unique and precious in its own way to the individual.

Emphasizing experience over possessions make some students feel that having a better life is now a more tangible proposition. Obtaining lots of money for possessions is a challenge, but rethinking experiences and having more good ones is something more of my students could actually get to fairly quickly, something that they can afford and create for themselves.

#72. Think this: Millions of people can be wrong. Not that: Millions of people can't be wrong.

A few years ago, one of my students challenged me on an idea when I said a lot of the stuff most people believed through advertisement was, in fact, not factual. He said, "You gotta be kiddin' me. Millions of people can't be wrong!"

I must admit, I don't like using value judgments statements, such as something being right or wrong, so I'll say that millions of people can miss it. The underlying assumption is that with millions of people agreeing on something, someone, somewhere had to have checked out the facts to see if everything is correct. Among humans, the opposite tends to be true, due to this thing called Group Think Fallacy. We presume wisdom in numbers. The problem is, everyone is assuming that, but no one is doing the work to verify the facts. In one of my South African Student Leadership courses at the University of Kwazulu-Natal, a student asked me about Group Think Fallacy and how that affects society as a whole. I informed her that coming from an advertising background, we often leveraged the "millions of people can't be wrong" idea as an extended form of our advertising effectiveness. The human need to meet the approval and admiration of peers drives people to swap their reasoning process out with the desire to be accepted. Group Think Fallacy is similar to peer pressure, except in this case you use the pride you feel in belonging to a group as a substitute for coming to a reasoned conclusion about some issue.

I submitted to my class that a lot of things they believe as true are merely myths they embraced because they saw it on television in some advertising or political campaign. No one likes being told that his/her ideas are not original, so there was resistance to what I said. So then I started naming some of the most popular expressions of group-think over the past 1000 years: the Crusades, European witch hunts of the Middle Ages, Nazism in Germany, China's Cultural Revolution, McCarthyism in the US, ethnic cleansing in the former Yugoslavia, the slaughter in Rwanda between the Hutus and Tutsis.... The list goes on.

We also did an exercise where one student would leave the room by my request (I'd ask them to go get me another dry erase marker). While that student was out, I'd draw four lines on the board and tell the students when I asked them how many lines were on the board, they would say three instead of four. When the student came back, I'd draw four lines on the board and ask "How many lines are there?" Per the instructions, the class would say three. I would ask the class three times the same question "How many lines are on the board?" Each time they would say three. Each time the student who was not part of the ruse would either say three or say nothing at all. In almost 10 years of doing this exercise, only one student ever stood up and said "Hey, wait, I see four lines." Everyone else wanted to go with the group.

I was listening to a conversation with Physicist and ESP researcher Russell Targ recently and the discussion focused on a periodic "cultural blind spot" that occurs at different times in every society. The United States has had more than a few of those, two of the more notorious being Manifest Destiny that led to the slaughter of millions of Native American people and Slavery, which also led to the death and enslavement of millions of Africans over a 250 year period. We abhor those events today with hindsight, but for hundreds of years, these two blind spots were thought of as perfectly logical and agreed to by millions of people. It is reasonable to evaluate our current society and ask, "What would be our cultural blind spot today?"

With the internet and the arrival of several data evaluation websites like FactCheck.org, everyone now has the ability to run a check of the facts as they stand. Things have changed. More information means more people informed. That sounds like a good thing.

#73. Think this: Whole Brain thinking can make us smarter. Not that: We only use 10% of our brain.

If you should ever go to an event and hear another motivational speaker give that classic line, "You're only using 10 percent of your brain," get up and leave. That person probably doesn't know what he/she is talking about. This classic conventional wisdom statement is not only outdated, it simply isn't true. "The 10-percent myth is so wrong it is almost laughable," says neurologist Barry Gordon at Johns Hopkins School of Medicine. Although there's no definitive culprit to pin the blame on for starting this legend, the notion has been linked to the American psychologist and author William James, who argued in *The Energies of Men* that "we are making use of only a small part of our possible mental and physical resources." It's also been associated with Albert Einstein, who supposedly used it to explain his cosmic towering intellect. So much for infallible intelligence.

Truth is, if we were not using all of our brain, we'd be comatose right about now. What is starting to emerge is an idea that we can do a better job of using both hemispheres of the brain more efficiently. The discipline is called "Whole Brain Learning." While there is a lot of pseudo science masquerading as new brain technology, Whole Brain Learning seems to be presenting the greatest promise and has weaved its way into popular culture. Whole Brain Learning is a technique to integrate our artistic talents in our right hemisphere with the more functional, bread-and-butter requirements of our left hemisphere. The theory is that if you use both sides of the brain in solving a challenge, you'll tap the power that both hemispheres contain to solve a problem. Here's an example: Play the music of Mozart or some early John Coltrane right before taking a standard IQ test. The right hemisphere somehow leverages the genius of these musicians to help the left brain think better. Another example: Use colored pens in a presentation. The right brain appreciates the colors while the left brain will remember the patterns, thus reinforcing the learning process.

I think you get the point.

We implement a number of simple whole brain training techniques in the class, including the "what is this circle on the board" exercise where the students each determined what they were seeing as well as the "filter" exercise where the students had to determine what kind of information they would allow in their sphere of influence. These are the tools students talk about when they leave the shelter and write me. "Remember that circle on the board exercise? I still remember that today." I'd remind them that was the whole purpose.

Despite all of our discoveries, the brain is still a mystery. However, one mystery of the brain that has been solved is how much of it is actually at work. All of it.

#74. Think this: These are the good old days. Not that: Those were the good old days.

Not too long ago, my youngest son and I had an extended conversation about rap music. He was sharing with me some of the hot groups and artists out now, and I shared with him stories and names from what is now known as "the golden age of rap/hip hop" (1987–1995). He told me about his peer set, from Lil' Wayne to TI and I told him about the people who laid the foundation for what he enjoys now, from Eric B and Rakim to Queen Latifah to A Tribe Called Quest. At the end of the discussion, I went back into that old familiar place that every older generation person lays on the youth—"Those were the good old days."

I realized that I started sounding like my father who used to always remind me that the stuff I was listening to was popcorn compared to what he listened to, which he referred to as "grown folks music." Every generation waxes poetically about the music, conditions and feeling of their earlier time, somehow leaving out the stuff that was just plain

159

crazy. The idea of "the good old days" buried somewhere in the past is part of the mythology and storytelling of almost every national and cultural group. When we go back to the earliest recordings of human history we find that the ancient Egyptians, Babylonians, Greeks or Hebrews all had their sacred stories of a golden age just as the Australian Aborigines have their Dreamtime. In more recent history, national or cultural groups have created their own golden age of noble beginnings.

Such is the case in a lot of our societies. When people go through difficult times, it becomes easy for them to romanticize a period of time that can be revised to fit an idea. It creates an escape so that the current challenge has context and is not overwhelming, even if it is a reconstructed context. For many humans, it's part of the process in managing difficulties.

This is the case with many of my students, particularly with young women who were going through breakups with abusive partners. After some time would elapse from being away from the abuser, they would begin to talk glowingly about the relationship and start to identify with the "good ole days" of the relationship.

In the United States, the period of time from the turn of the 20th century until about 1965 is often referred to as "the good old days." But once you pull the curtain back and look at the stats, another America emerges. That time was not so golden for African Americans who lived as second-class citizens in a world that was dangerous and potentially deadly at any given time. World War I, World War II, The Korean

Conflict and the Vietnam War were part of that time period. Let's not leave out the Cold War and the development of the atomic bomb. Shall we talk about the unrelenting exploitation of the environment and natural resources that we're now paying for today? Of course, exploiting other human beings was par for the course as well. There was also unreported spousal abuse, child abuse, lynching, and race riots. Yes, despite what modern conventional wisdom may say about us living in a more dangerous time, FBI records from those years compared to now show a mirror reflection in the crime rate. By the early 70s it was the same as in the 30s—but no worse. There was a definitive uptick in crime during the mid 1980s, but after the early 90s it dropped again as the crack epidemic subsided. Today it's about the same as in the mid-60s. The murder rate doesn't exactly match point for point the overall violent crime rate, of course. Still, in some ways the 1920s and 1930s were as dangerous as now.

Read what Princeton historian Lawrence Stone says about the period 1890–1920 here in the U.S.

> *The almost total ignorance of both personal and public hygiene meant that the contamination of food and water were constant hazards. The result of these primitive sanitary conditions was constant outbursts of bacterial stomach infections, the most fearful of all being dysentery, which swept away many victims of both sexes and of all ages within a few hours or days.... The prevalence of intestinal worm were a slow, disgusting and debilitating disease that caused a vast amount of misery and*

ill-health.... Another fact of Early Modern life which is easy to forget is that only a relatively small proportion of the adult population at any given time was both healthy and attractive, quite apart from the normal features of smell and dirt.... Both sexes must very often have had a bad breath from the rotting teeth and constant stomach disorders, which can be documented from many sources, while suppurating ulcers, eczema, scabs, running sores and other nauseating skin diseases were extremely common and often lasted for years.

Yikes! That's probably why they shook hands instead of hugged.

Our ability to admit that sometimes our recall of the facts from the past can distort our perception of what actually happened is important for two reasons: First, it keeps us from drifting into repeated cycles. Second, it gives us context for what we want to create for the future. With the young ladies in my class who were victims of abuse, identifying this tendency allowed them to first see that unless they saw the abuse for what it was, they would seek out another partner just like the one they ran from. It would also allow them to more accurately identify what kind of partner that was best for them going forward.

At the risk of sounding a bit preachy, generations into the future may look back at this time and say these truly were the good old days—not because things were so nice, but because we acted with intention as we looked toward the future.

#75. Think this: There was pre-Columbian contact with people in the Americas. Not that: Columbus "discovered" America.

Sometimes it is difficult getting through to my students about some of the problems that exist in some of their old thinking. Some fight back against my suggestions that they need to review long held beliefs. One of the most explosive and sensitive concepts the students struggle to grasp is my challenging the conventional wisdom about Christopher Columbus. Here is the information I share with them that they find so volatile:

1. Columbus did not set out to prove the world was round. The general assumption of his time was that the world was round, not flat.

2. Columbus incorrectly assumed a significantly smaller diameter for Earth, claiming that Asia, particularly India, could be easily reached by sailing west across the Atlantic. So he named the people of the Caribbean "Indians" thinking he had arrived in India. The name stuck for all native people of the Americas.

3. Columbus did not land in what is now called The United States of America, in 1492. He landed in what is now called The Bahamas. He never made it to continental North America.

Even more, there were several groups that did reach the New World and made contact with the native peoples well before Columbus. New evidence shows Chinese Admiral Cheng Ho arrived in America in 1421. In 1963, a Viking-like settlement was discovered in Newfoundland, dating back to the year AD 1000. Indian scholar R. A. Jairazbhoy states that the earliest settlers in the Caribbean were Ancient Egyptians led by King Rameses III, during the 19th dynasty. West African artifacts, skulls and legends were discovered in Mezo America by the new Spanish explorers when they arrived. The mounting evidence is that no one "discovered" America, but several groups made contact with the people already there. Columbus was given credit because he had better PR.

It is becoming increasingly out of step to speak of Columbus in the context of noble hero of the new world, especially in light of damning reports of how he treated native peoples, especially on Hispaniola where he was appointed governor. This is not to take away from his courage and foresight in adventure, but to put it in historical context. His story is a classic example of how bits and pieces of information can grow into conventional wisdom, then morph into a narrative that we teach in classrooms and create holidays around.

#76. Think this: The woman came first. Not that: Man came first.

Last year, I was a presenter at a world youth conference in Malaysia. The theme for the conference was gender equality and the role of youth going forward. My subject was that the Economic and Environmental Sustainability movement must be tied to the gender equality movement because it is impossible to talk about better managing our resources for sustainability without talking about the biggest, best and most under utilized resource we have: women. This conference was dominated by youth from a number of Islamic countries and emerging countries that held traditional "women second" beliefs. Much to my delight, the young people were adamant about gender equality and wanted a different look at the role of women in the world going forward. If things are changing in these countries, things are changing.

And they are, especially in our rethinking of the "man came first" idea that is the foundation for some cultures to enforce gender inequality.

With apologies to the religions that support a "man first" hypothesis, new genetic data say it was Adam who may have come from Eve's rib...at least with modern human beings.

Peter Underhill and colleagues at Stanford University say men and women have "different molecular clocks. Fewer men participated in reproduction than women did."

His team, working with top geneticists across the United States, Europe, Israel and Africa, did a genetic analysis of DNA samples from the Y chromosomes of more than 1,000 men from 22 geographic areas and determined that their most recent common ancestor was a man who lived in Africa around 59,000 years ago.

Only men have Y chromosomes and researchers can look at gradual genetic mutations in them to "count" generations.

Other studies have used mitochondrial DNA, which women seem to pass down virtually unchanged from mother to daughter, to show that the genetic "Eve" lived 143,000 years ago.

The latest study, published in the journal Nature Genetics, reconciles the two findings, and in the process the researchers came up with new tool for looking at how people are different from one another genetically.

Hopefully, some of this information will help end practices in some countries where women are abused and mistreated, simply because they are believed to be second class citizens.

#77. Think this: The lack of ethics is the root of all evil. Not that: The love of money is the root of all evil.

Saying the love of money is the root of all evil is a cheap shot. People want money to help them live the life that they want, so their desire or "love" for it doesn't make them evil. In many of my seminars around the world and with classes at the shelter, rich people became primary targets for anger. I think the focus on money obscures the fact that there are knuckleheads across the socioeconomic landscape. I've always told my class if you're a low ball when you're poor, you'll be a low ball when you're rich. It's not the money, it's the person and their commitment to an ethical standard that is affirmative and empowering...or not.

Over the past few years, the world has experienced a series of high profile ethics scandals, bringing down some high profile people, exploiting thousands of innocent customers, parishioners and devotees. The money didn't cause the scandal. It's what the people did with the money or resources that caused the mess. Some societies are responding by introducing Spirituality in the Workplace. I had an invitation to present a workshop in Montreux, Switzerland on Workplace Spirituality. I've discovered this is one of the hottest topics in the world today. The ongoing ethics crises have company leaders looking for ways of keeping their employees morally upright as well as visionary. There is a trend in bringing in a Spiritual Director to help a company find its moral bearings, which has been growing steadily since the late 1980s. It seems to be working. Ian Mitroff, co-author of *A Spiritual Audit of Corporate America* writes that those individuals who work in organizations in which their moral values are supported through a corporate spiritual openness are likely to be more productive and less likely and to be susceptible to employment offers from other companies.

My own introduction of spirituality in the classes turned out to be a great tool for helping students see beyond immediate self-gratification and view what they do from a bigger place. How will what I do impact my family? How will I be remembered once I pass away? What is one thing I have done that has benefited others? This kind of discussion isn't something to be reserved for some college philosophy class. This is stuff everyday people should be contemplating, too.

When talking about money, an old friend of mine used to say, "It's not about the car, it's about whose driving the car that determines where it will go". It appears the new conventional wisdom is putting the focus where it belongs... on the driver.

#78. Think this: Soft power works effectively. Not that: Power and might work effectively.

One lesson I teach is helping students to negotiate better in the world. They often see themselves as people who want to get something from people who have something. I change the discussion and show them the best negotiating position is to see yourself as someone who has something and is prepared to offer it at a decent rate to those who need it. In a sense, you become the solution for their problem. So the emphasis in the class is not to look for a job, but to find people who had a problem that you had the solution to. This "give" instead of "get" position is the new reality of soft power.

Soft power is the ability to obtain what one wants through cooperation and attraction. It is in contradistinction to "absolute power," which is the use of coercion and payment.

I like to think of it in the way I managed negotiations in my first marriage. My wife of the time would often have "tasks" for me to do with her on Sunday afternoon. Of course, that's when the NFL games were broadcast. I became wise to her plans and started spending my entire Saturday with our children in the afternoon and the night with her, on the town, or doing whatever she wanted. When it came time for me to have Sunday afternoons to myself so that I could watch the games, I had *carte blanche.*

Booya. Soft power in action.

Helping people to get what they want so you can get what you want reduces stress and expands your influence. My students now look at job interviewing from a completely different place.

#79. Think this: Presence, presence, presence. Not that: Location, location, location.

I spend a lot of time talking to the students about how the new technologies have changed the game. The playing field hasn't been leveled, but it's definitely been made more accessible. I tell students that even if they don't take advantage of the new playing field, they should at least know that they're not automatically excluded from playing. In the days when money was king, any business person will tell you that if you have the right location for your operation, you pretty much ruled the day. These Big Money people could pretty much take their ball and go home if they didn't like the way the game was going. The new playing field is creating a different kind of rule—if you have good presence, you can rule the day, no matter where you are in the world. So even if the kid with all the money takes his ball and goes home, you can create your own game and have a great time.

Location is becoming a moot point.

Yes, if you have a challenge with incontinence, the location of where the bathrooms are IS important. The reason things are changing is the internet. This tool of the 21st century changes the game when it comes to business in particular. It allows you to locate your operations anywhere in the world and still have great communications with your clients and relationships with people everywhere. This can be especially helpful when cost is a factor. Perfect case in point is high-end clothing maker Ted Baker. Although British fashion brands are supposed to start in London, where they can build street cred, the Ted Baker company opted to start in Glasgow. He valued lower rents and the right ambiance above the high-rent district.

At this writing, I'm in negotiations with the University of Namibia to provide online classes covering conventional wisdom and leadership via Skype from the privacy of my Denver condo. Your new market is not just the places in proximity to where you are. Your new market is where you have presence.

Presence is the key.

I help my students realize this more directly by creating

a three-step internet presence as they were looking for a job.

1. Post a Craigslist ad offering your skills at a decent rate.
2. Set up a simple website that tells potential employers what work skills you can provide for them.
3. Apply for day labor jobs online.

Our shelter allows residents to go online pretty regularly. We are helping the students to maximize their presence in the field and increase the odds of employment success.

#80. Think this: Discretion is a better policy. Not that: Honesty is the best policy.

Ever meet people who use honesty as a weapon? I had students like that. They told what was on their mind in class every time they had the opportunity. It seemed as though they were using this honesty to get maximum shock value and, in some cases, violate the sensibilities of their fellow classmates. Don't get me wrong, it was the truth, but there is this thing called TMI that this student didn't quite appreciate. So, I created a study stream about discretion and honesty.

In forming this lesson plan, I often thought of my parents and their different styles. My mom is very honest with me about things to do, what not to do, how people are, etc. I could always trust her to give it to me straight. She gave me these skills of how to live in the world. My father had a big picture, philosophical, discreet look at things. His philosophy taught me how to be in the world. Both of their approaches worked. The honesty my mom gives me I keep in my heart. My father's emphasis on discretion taught me how to take my mom's honesty and use it as a personal tool for navigating life, then use diplomacy, wisdom and thoughtfulness when dealing with others.

We incorporate these values in the class so that the students think through their decisions, the way they talk to their employers, how they handle domestic challenges and how to decipher what others say to them.

As with all of these classes, I never got "too deep" on my students. We keep it simple by role playing and imagining scenarios.

#81. Think this: Love is more than a feeling. Not that: Love is a feeling.

Every year around Valentines Day I do a special "Love" class. This class focuses on understanding what love really is. This class is always a hit because the students are genuinely looking for insight into the thing that brought many of them into homelessness in the first place—an abusive or financially ruinous significant other. The lesson plan for this class is to get the students to know these basics:

1. Love is always a decision. You choose to love someone.

2. Opposites may attract, but they don't necessarily make for strong relationships.

3. Not being afraid to disagree with the person means the relationship has roots.

4. It's an excellent sign when you laugh together.

5. Both of you are okay when you have times of being silent around each other.

I am an Officiant in the state of Colorado, so I marry people all the time. It's one of those things that I just love. Prior to the wedding I do an interview with the couple to find out where they are. These are the same talking points I bring up during that interview. It helps all of us get a better idea of what's going on in the relationship.

Shift Tool 7

Paying Attention To The Ordinary Leads To Extraordinary Insight.

My mom and my grandmother share May birthdays, so the opportunity came for me to celebrate my mom's 70th and to mark my grandmother's 89th in one fell swoop. It was over a year since I had seen them, so I was eager to get back and let them know how things were turning out for me. Upon my arrival, my mom and I went through our usual game of catch up—trying desperately to cram months of things going on in our lives into every waking moment we had with each other. Mom and I are both talkers (but my mom could wipe the floor with me in a talking contest) so you can imagine a steady stream of non-stop conversation that happened between us. As we went further into the conversation, I shared news on the success I was having speaking and teaching around the country and overseas. I told her about how well my books were selling and the number of classes that had emerged using *The Window Effect Method*. She smiled and said "That's nice, but I've got some bushes that need some trimmin' and some weeds that need pullin'. Can you do that?" I smiled and said "Yes, ma'am. I can." That Saturday morning, with saw and weed eater in hand, I went to work under my mom's supervision and conversation.

My mom was able to bring me right back home to something very fundamental in the human experience. Our greatest selves are not made during our "highlight reels"—those precious moments when we defy the odds and overcome obstacles to do things the world would recognize as great. Those moments are nice and I wouldn't begrudge them. But it has become clear to me that those moments are simply the by-products of the work that was done in the mundane, the obscure, the everyday. In a loud and demonstrative society, the "everyday things" are often sacrificed, and often at great cost to insight and understanding.

Pay attention. Keep it simple. Chop the wood. Carry the water. Trim the bushes. Pull the weeds.

Trends

#82. Think this: Slow is good. Not that: Fast is good.

Ever feel you need a break from your fast-paced life? Spend time at a homeless shelter. I'm serious.

Many of my students speak of their time at the shelter as being a break from a life that was driving them crazy because of the pace. As tough as being in the shelter is, the students say they're finally getting a chance to breathe and regroup simply because life slowed down. That got me thinking, how fast is too fast when it comes to our basic sanity? I've discovered a lot of other people are asking that question, too. Enter the emerging Slow Movement.

One of the most significant developments lately has been the Slow Food movement. The movement, created for people who could no longer "stomach" the idea of fast food, is international and founded by Carlo Petrini in 1986. It strives to preserve traditional and regional cuisine and promotes farming of plants, seeds and livestock characteristics of the local ecosystem. There is also the "Africa Time" movement that has taken off since the year 2000. This idea is to value, not demonize, the common belief that Africans hold a polychronic view of time, where time is not linear or sequential and not fully determined by punctuality. The Slow Travel movement emerged during the 1990s as a way to make vacations a way to break from fast-paced lives rather than extending them. Take Back Your Time, a nonprofit group based in Seattle, Washington, is leading a national campaign to address time famine by using conferences and teach-ins to wean people from their need by be busy. The Long Now Foundation, a group based in San Francisco, California, was established to provide an alternative to a "faster/cheaper" mind set and promote "slower/better" thinking.

In the class, I help students configure their new schedules differently so that it isn't the action-packed time cruncher that brought them into the shelter in the first place. I also talk about how to manage a slower-paced life for success in a fast-paced world. It's not as hard as you might think. The key to this re-tooling is to remind the student to do one thing at a time.

#83. Think this: Small is beautiful. Not that: Bigger is better.

When people come into homeless shelters, there are some ideas they're willing to take a look at and reconsider to see if it works for them. Then there are those ideas they would consider "not reviewable." "Bigger is better" has traditionally been one of those "not reviewables."

Sometime in the 1990s the conventional wisdom of bigger is better seemed to move from something we kinda thought about to an idea on crack. Now, living beyond our means, widespread waste and concern for environmental sustainability is forcing us to live more efficiently. As a result we're backing off big. Hummers look a lot less like golden chariots than dinosaurs. Driving a hybrid or electric car is the new status symbol. Developers burned by an ice-cold real estate market are downsizing their projects and, in the emerging countries throughout Asia and Africa, big plans are being draw up for smaller homes for working families. Even our mobile phones are now rolling up various other devices into one small package. It's being called The Small Movement.

The first time I truly noticed this movement was back in the 1990s when my then wife and I went to Paris, the City of Lights, to have our delayed honeymoon since we had eloped. In fact, it was April in Paris. We toured the Champs Elysees, the Eiffel Tower, and the Louvre, but spent most of our time in a very cool, casual boutique hotel. It was my first time being in a room not much bigger than the kitchen at home. The more I travelled around Europe, Africa and Asia, the more I realized how large, expansive homes were not the norm. That is a distinctly American idea. We've viewed smaller homes, cars, companies, etc., as something less than prosperous and successful. We've developed a religion around big. Big companies, megachurches, expansive homes, oversized SUVs and automobiles. Even our waistlines are big. Everything is big.

From The Small Plate Movement at restaurants, to the Small Home Movement by developers as well as the Small

School Movement by educators and, yes, even the Small Dog Movement, everyone is discovering a new kind of wisdom about size. My thinking is that if I want to prepare my students for success in a changing world, you give them real time data. The real time data says thinking small will make them more successful.

During the height of the Bail Out programs for major banks and financial institutions in the United States, Pastor Rick Warren's megachurch in Southern California was having a financial meltdown of its own. The church was short by a little more than a million dollars and couldn't meet expenses. It sent a letter out to parishioners asking for help. They came through to the tune of over 2 million dollars. I mentioned this to a Christian friend of mine and made the wry remark, "Now it seems even churches are in the market for a bailout. Are the megachurches too big to fail?" He didn't appreciate my humor and took offense. He told me that the work Pastor Warren is doing is commendable and that they deserved the support so that they could continue doing this most important work. Then he pulled what he perceived as a trump card on me and said "Look at all of the great work their church is doing in Africa. That takes money!" I replied, "It doesn't take millions of dollars—just willing spirits. I've been doing work in Africa for the past seven years conducting workshops on Sustainable Society Leadership and I've been doing it, most of the time, at my own expense and on a shoestring. I've been doing it without a paid staff of hundreds or massive overhead."

He fired back: "What Pastor Warren is doing is what Jesus has commanded us to do."

I replied, "Last I read, Jesus didn't need a megachurch to do his work. It was just him and 12 associates. I think we need to make sure that we recognize the idea of big, megachurches is a contemporary idea and truly something born out of our culture. We think because we honor the idea of big is better, God must also think that way. That's where we are blurring the lines between our cultural selves and our religious selves." We just agreed to disagree.

One of the groovy things about smaller is that the odds increase you'll not live beyond your means trying to keep up with the Joneses. Smaller can be cheaper, and that is very good news for my students in transition. The last thing they need is to get back into a culture of conspicuous consumption in an effort to gain some respect.

Another cool thing about people in transition is that, for many of them, all of their worldly possessions have been taken away. Starting from scratch makes the path to change a lot easier than if you had to part with things. At this point, all they had to do is rethink an idea.

Yes, size does matter, but in a way where sustainability is the first and foremost consideration. Small is beautiful, baby.

Chet W. Sisk

#84. Think this: The world is becoming underpopulated. Not that: The world is overpopulated.

I throw this out to my students just to blow their minds.

Doesn't quite seem right, doesn't it? The idea that the world may not have enough people goes against all of those legends we've been told since we were kids. Most of the literature and conventional wisdom for the past 100 years regularly and consistently told tales of the population boom that would eventually doom all of humankind as we all fight over limited resources. Part of that discussion is true. We are fighting over limited resources, but the resources are not limited because of too many people, but rather, terrible management due to geopolitical manipulation. The truth is, we're not even close to over population in the world.

Some Environmentalist have been running around with the over population war cry because they often see humans as evil in comparison to the rest of nature. Some conservatives have been whipping up hype about this as a way to keep other cultures out of their countries. But, in truth, the world is a big place with plenty of space. Allow me to provide some perspective in relation to the 6.5 billion people in the world at this writing. Consider the small nation of Japan. It has about 143,000 square miles of area. One square mile has $5,280 * 5,280 = 27.9$ million square feet. Japan has a total of about 4 trillion square feet, enough to give each person of the earth 670 square feet. If we housed people in families of four in simple two-level buildings (8 people per building, one family of four per level), each building could be on a lot of over 5,300 square feet. If we used the American average of 8,000 square feet to four people, the entire population of the planet would fit into a space as big as Texas and Nevada combined—leaving the rest of the land for food production and entertainment venues. Where most of us get twisted is if we live in major urban areas. Humans like to cluster in tight spaces. The jobs are there, the entertainment is there and other people are there. If you live in a congested city filled with millions of people, yes, the world does seem extremely overpopulated. But just go a few kilometers outside of town and you'll see space all around you.

The challenge of the 21st century will be under population. One of the best books written on this is the 2005 release *Fewer: How the New Demography of Depopulation Will Shape Our Future*, by Ben Wattenberg. His argument is straight and clear: fertility rates in virtually all countries in the world have fallen further and faster than anyone could have imagined just a few years ago. World population is no longer exploding, and will soon be shrinking. The truth is, most Western countries have been at zero population growth for some time, and a 2009 article in *The Economist* shows that African, Asian and South American countries are now following suit.

Let me offer a caveat for those of you who think this argument is complete rubbish. It is true, people do tend to abuse our natural resources disproportionately as compared to all other living creatures on the planet. But the challenge is not with the numbers as much as it is with our habits. The sustainability movement knows this and is addressing it directly.

In many places around the world, the conventional wisdom of overpopulation is driving debates on immigration. With coming labor shortages because of fewer people, the under population conventional wisdom will drive the debate, too.

#85. Think this: You need at least some secondary education to make it in the world. Not that: You need at least a high school diploma to make it in the world.

The temptation among some care workers is to teach down to our students and clients because there is an assumption that they don't have the capacity to comprehend heavy- duty knowledge. We listen to the way they speak, how they dress, the places they go and figure, "They're just not that smart."

My experience has been that many of the people we assume are not very bright are simply acting out part of a "group think" support system. They have the tools to know more, but their environment doesn't support expanded capacity as being helpful, necessary or important. In my classroom, we create an artificial environment that says higher thought and expanded capacity is the rule. The students respond accordingly. This became particularly noticeable to me when I started emphasizing the importance of getting secondary education and how so many students voiced, some for the first time, their desire to get secondary education. I would emphasize the benefits of obtaining secondary education or training and pair it with the threat of what could happen if they don't get more learning. They could get left behind.

Be it college, trade school or technical training, the world has evolved beyond the simple high school diploma. This is not just a family pride thing, where your parents can tell their friends about the strides you've made in achieving educational goals ... this is about the trend around the world where employers must have skilled workers to manage in a much more technically advanced environment. Practically all jobs are being "upskilled." The technical workforce is growing in size and importance and few of us will be able to escape that fact. According to Joseph Boyett's *21st Century Work Trends*, workers with strong technical skills—lab technicians, computer professionals, drafters, paralegals, medical technicians, designers, engineers, and so on—are becoming the front-line workers of most organizations. Even jobs that have not traditionally been considered technical positions, such as a courier, have a strong technical component and require the use of computers and other sophisticated electronic devices. At the same time, the semiskilled and unskilled jobs that employed masses of illiterate or semiliterate workers in the past are disappearing at a rapid pace.

This change is affecting our conventional wisdom about the high school diploma, the one-time hallmark of learning for the average person in the 20th century. The high school diploma may soon be seen in the same way of graduating from grade school—it's a great ceremonial event, but there's more you have to do to be a competent, functioning adult in the world.

#86. Think this: We are moving toward a meaning society. Not that: We are in the information society.

Often students wax philosophical and ask me, "What does all of this madness mean, Chet? Why are we here?" I respond, "One of the most powerful things you've done in this life is ask that question out loud. Most people aren't even asking the question."

Here we are in a tidal wave of information, but we know less. The reason? We're not seeking meaning—just data. In an information society, data means everything. But as we're starting to notice, data means nothing without meaning. This loss of meaning is what some would call our inability to extract purpose, knowledge and wisdom from the tons of information we're inundated with every day. Failing education systems, a breakdown in ethics and morals, extremist partisanship and corruption throughout the society as evidence of this.

Suddenly, there are tons of books emerging on this very subject. Some of them include: *The Shallows: What The Internet Is Doing To Our Brains* by Nicholas Carr, *True Enough: Learning To Live In A Post-Fact Society* by Farhaad Manjoo, and *Idiot America: How Stupidity Became A Virtue* by Charles P. Pierce.

Even before these books, a prophetic movie in 1976 called *Network* spoke of how our instant information world could lead to loss of meaning and clarity of the facts. Below is an excerpt from that movie, read by the character, Howard Beale, as played by actor Peter Finch. In the movie, he's the host of his own television show, now addressing a live television audience:

So you listen to me. Listen to me. Television is not the truth. Television's a goddamned amusement park.... We're in the boredom-killing business. So if you want the truth, go to God. Go to your gurus. Go to yourselves. Because that's the only place you're ever going to find any real truth. But, man, you're never gonna get any truth from us. We'll tell you anything you wanna hear.

We lie like hell.... We'll tell you any shit you want to hear. We deal in illusions, man. None of it is true. But you people sit there, day after day, night after night, all ages, colors, creeds. We're all you know. You're beginning to believe the illusions we're spinning. You're beginning to think the tube is reality and your lives are unreal.

You do whatever the tube tells you. You dress like the tube, eat like the tube, raise your children like the tube, think like the tube.

This is mass madness, you maniacs. In God's name, you people are the real thing! We are the illusion!

You've got to rent the movie. A little something gets lost in the translation with just text!

Not only are there books emerging to address the issue of meaning, there are groups springing up all over the world to help us process this tidal wave of info and images. I've mentioned before the Commons Movement that seeks to simplify life and democratize our institutions. Awareness Into Action is having great success getting professionals into the Sustainability Movement. And in a 2008 *New York Times* report, the number of young people enrolling in philosophy as a major is increasing. Nationwide, there are more colleges offering undergraduate philosophy programs today than a decade ago (817, up from 765), according to the College Board.

I didn't overwhelm my students in this area of finding meaning, but I did give them some basics in understanding that information is not meaning and that they should lean more heavily on their intuitive knowledge to help navigate the world. That still small voice can speak volumes if we're willing to listen.

#87. Think this: I'm planning for my Third Life. Not that: I'm planning my retirement.

When life expectancy in many parts of the world hovered around 40 years, retirement wasn't even a consideration. As life expectancy increased, societies had to rethink the role elderly people play. Germany was the first country to create retirement back in the late 1800s. Now, it's conventional wisdom to talk about retiring from the work force after you reach a certain age.

The problem with retirement in modern societies is that everyone doesn't want to go play golf or bingo and be shuffled off to a retirement community. Many people want to continue their lives, not only for financial reasons, but for peace of mind and feeling like a contributing member of society.

Many of my more elderly students all but gave up on doing something with their lives. They just wanted to find a safe place to curl up and watch television. Noticing this prompted me to start to teach about Third Life.

After youth, there's adulthood, then there's Third Life. Third Life is focused around utilizing senior years to becoming a key contributor to the world, and not retire from it. Retirement specialists are now starting to advise their middle aged clients about Third Life and how to plan for it.

That being said, let me share with you some information I gathered from some of the leading retirement experts in the field of what they believe their clients should consider in Third Life:

Consult: My grandmother and grandfather started a church back in the 1960s. My grandfather was the pastor. He has since passed away, but his legacy remains. The new pastor regularly consults my grandmother for her Biblical understanding and motherly wisdom. She is more than happy to share the wisdom she's gained from her 92 years on earth. She is a consultant for the church and is compensated for her knowledge. Your insight has a value to any organization you've spent some time with. Leverage it.

Write: The internet is creating multiple online and offline opportunities for people who want to share information without having to leave the comfort of their home.

Convert your hobby into an income generator. One of the coolest guys I ever met in the world was an elderly dude who farmed in his back yard and took his organic bounty to the farmer's market. He loves doing it and he makes a tidy amount. Whatever it is you enjoy doing, there's a market for it, somewhere.

World service: I recently discovered this organization called Mediators Without Borders. All they do is help people settle disputes in the world. My guess is that people near retirement age have seen their share of conflicts and disputes and could possible put their insight to use to make the world a better place. There are many opportunities like this. You just have to ask around.

Voluntourism: This growing trend combines volunteering in exotic places around the world with a vacation in that place. It's being promoted as a Sustainable form of vacation where the tourist gives back as much as they get. How cool would it be to teach children in Belize, then tour the Mayan pyramids all during the same trip. I saw the pyramids. They're stunning.

Teach: Community colleges, high schools, grade

schools, technical institutes—there are tons of opportunities to teach. They may not always be good paying gigs, but they can lead to some income generation and an opportunity to share what you know.

Become a student again: The plus-65 crowd may actually be smarter than the rest of us. In "The Secret Life of the Grown-Up Brain," *New York Times* deputy science editor Barbara Strauch says that not only do human beings keep their existing brain cells intact throughout their middle-age years but new ones also continue to form, according to the U.K.'s *Daily Mail*. That would suggest that perhaps older people are better students and better learners.

In many African cultures, there is no such thing as retirement. On the contrary, once you reach a certain age, you're expected to step up and help guide the culture with your experience. It's called Eldership. Often these elders preside at weddings, baby blessings, funerals, Rites of Passage events and other life changing moments. They are often paid out of a community fund. Perhaps in the US, this new push about Third Life will take some of the pressure off our stressed entitlement programs.

Shift Tool 8 — *Expanding Capacity By Breaking Patterns*

We all have patterns of thought in our minds that we have been building all of our lives. In advertising, we counted on those patterns to kick in and eventually turn into brand loyalty for our product. For example we learn to recognize and name aspects of experience—both tangible aspects like "car" or "factory" and intangible aspects like "passion" or "development." These patterns of experience also include non-nameable and sometimes extremely complex patterns. For instance, we may make decisions about investment in development without being able to put our finger on why we believe it is necessary or why it will work out well.

Many of the deeper patterns are fixed and forgotten—for instance, how to ride a bicycle. We forget why we behave in certain ways and sometimes the way we behave is more driven by forgotten patterns than by current circumstances. In other areas we are constantly shifting patterns and experimenting with re-arrangements—we continue to learn.

Those pattern methods are designed to make it easy for us to assume—that is, make sense of a lot of information quickly. This is called passive thinking. Obviously, this pattern recognition skill can save us in case there is danger, but it can also limit us if we want to create new thought, new ideas and new possibilities. Before someone out there demonizes pattern thinking, let me say that it is dangerous to throw out the baby with the bath water. Pattern recognition may have saved our lives on many different occasions throughout life. What we want to do is recognize that it exists so we can create a conscious addendum to this agenda: a way of breaking through the patterns to expand our capacity and keeping our ability to make sense of the world around us. Here are three things you can do right now to start expanding your thinking capacity and possibilities:

1. Whenever you go to the grocery store, pick up one magazine from the magazine rack. Make it a magazine you would not otherwise read. Make the time to read or even skim through (if your time is really tight) the magazine in one week. Do this every week for two months. You could even continue this as a life pattern. You are inviting yourself into worlds you would otherwise miss.

2. Turn on the television and watch it, with the sound turned off, for one hour. You will start to notice human behavior subtleties often missed with the sound up. Do this for at least a week.

3. Call a family member and ask them about your family tree. This helps you to get past your own personal stereotype about who you really are.

The key here is to challenge the assumptions of your mental patterns. Without breaking past those patterns, you will become a prisoner to them. Expanded capacity is the birthplace of possibilities.

Shift Tool 9

The Vision Party/Focus Group

In advertising, we would often gather a representative group of people from our target demographic, get them together in a room, and ask them specific questions our product. These groups would give us specific insight as to how our product is being received to the people we're trying to sell to.

You can do something similar by creating your own personal focus group. This group, however, is not necessarily designed to measure your product. It's designed as a group where you can share your particular dream and get feedback on how to make the dream happen. Most people don't talk about their dream, and those who do, don't share it beyond a few confidential friends. This process, the Vision Party/ Focus Group allows you to get the encouragement you need to step into unknown territory outside of conventional wisdom, and more information you may not have thought about before. This practice was particularly highly effective among homeless individuals.

There are, however, rules to who may participate in your vision party/focus group:

1. Keep the number small. 10 is a good set.

2. This is not the place for criticism. You'll get enough of that along the way. Remind the invited that you're looking for support and ideas, not critical analysis.

3. Get people you would not normally contact. If you keep going back to the same people you've always consulted, you'll get the same results. Open things up with new blood.

4. Make sure you have your idea clear before the gathering. This will help the participants provide you with clear advice.

5. Have the participants write down their comments

when they share them so that you have some record you can review later.

6. Break out the wine and cheese. Okay, that's what I would do. If you are averse to the grape, water will do. Just make sure you feed folk at your gathering. You don't want them leaving hungry. They'll talk about you.

Conclusion

How I arrived at becoming a life skills teacher at a homeless shelter may not have been of my choosing, but my decision to stay and spend the past 9 years of my life definitely was. A rule that I've grown to live by is that people stay in a situation by their choosing because they're getting something out of it. I can truly say I have been getting back as much as I have been giving. Probably more.

What I've shared with you in this book is only a tip of the iceberg of so many pieces of information that came to me in this process of helping people in transition live a better life. I know there are a lot of books out there that talk about changing people's lives. What separates this one from them is:

- It goes beyond theory to practical application.
- It's real-world tested
- It's tested on the toughest audience out there—people in the middle of the most challenging times of their lives.

My belief is that the job of the teacher is to wipe the film off of the lens so that the student has a clearer vision. My hope is that this book shows that particular relationship between me and the students I've spent so many of my adult years with.

I'm convinced that our ability as people to step away from conventional wisdom that has held us down for so long is critical. The longer we allow the tyranny of old, archaic thought to run the house, the more the house will fall into decay and ruin. It doesn't have to be this way.

I don't profess to say that changing up our thinking is an easy task. On the contrary, it's the hardest thing we'll ever do, but it's also the greatest thing. Once we examine that which we have believed, we may find ourselves changing some thought pattern. Once we change some of those thoughts patterns, we'll change our attitude. Once we change our attitude, we'll go into some kind of action.

Use this book as a reference guide as you continue on your own path of clarity, insight and vision. I'll be joining you on that path myself.

See ya on the road....

Look for *Think This, Not That, Too.*

About The Author

Chet W. Sisk is the proud middle son of James and Naomi Sisk. Their two names combined, James and Naomi, make up the name of the publishing company that produced this book, Jasina Media WorldWide, of which Chet is the president.

Chet is the father of the two brightest stars in the universe—Chet Mario Sisk and Chase Maliq Langston Sisk.

When not writing, Chet is either Salsa dancing, teaching at the Samaritan House Homeless Shelter in Denver, travelling the world, holding Sustainable Leadership Workshops or listening to the personal stories of people he never knew before. This gives him perspective as a journalist and writer.

Chet founded the Quality Foods For Everyone program to provide high-quality, organic and natural foods to homeless people. $2 from the purchase of each book will go towards purchasing these foods for homeless shelters around the country. Chet is a strong believer in Social Entrepreneurship, where people and profits go hand in hand. In Chet's own words: "We can do well and do good in the world. It is our charge."

To contact Chet for speaking engagements or to find out more about the Quality Foods For Everyone program, go to www.chetsisk.com or e-mail him directly at chet@chetsisk.com.

LaVergne, TN USA
18 October 2010
201208LV00002B/1/P